# first world war
# poems

**Dedication**

To Louy, with love, and in memory
of my grandfathers, Jack and Dickie,
whom I sadly never knew, but who both fought in this war.

First published in the United Kingdom in 2014 by
National Trust Books
10 Southcombe Street, London W14 0RA

An imprint of Pavilion Books Group Ltd

ISBN: 9781909881105

A CIP catalogue record for this book is available from
the British Library.

Colour reproduction by Mission Productions, Hong Kong
Printed by Toppan Leefung Printing Ltd, China
Design by Lee-May Lim

This book can be ordered direct from the publisher at
the website www.anovabooks com, or try your local
bookshop. Also available at National Trust shops and
www.nationaltrust.org.uk/shop

# first world war
# poems

Edited by
Jane McMorland Hunter

**National Trust**

**Editor's Acknowledgements**

I would like to thank Peter Taylor at National Trust Books and, as always, my agent Teresa Chris. Much of my research was done at the Saison Poetry Library at the Royal Festival Hall. Set in the heart of London, overlooking the Thames, this library has an amazing collection of books, excellent resources online, wonderfully helpful staff and is a joy to use.

Many people helped me compile this anthology, in particular, David and Louy Piachaud got me started and Sally Hughes increased my interest in the First World War. Jeremy Bourne, Simon Darragh, Charlotte Dickerson, Sue Gibb, Toby Piachaud, Kate Rae and Louise Simson all made helpful suggestions. Jeanie Bankler-Jukes and Alexia Coronini provided invaluable help at various stages and John and Teresa Simson kindly allowed me to include the two poems by Eric Simson.

Most of all, huge thanks to David Gibb, whose encouragement and firm eye made this anthology both fascinating and inspiring to compile.

Over the years I have collected many anthologies of First World War poetry. In particular, I would recommend the following:
*Men who March Away* edited by I. M. Parsons
*Scars Upon my Heart: Women's Poetry and Verse of the First World War* edited by Catherine Reilly
*Never Such Innocence* edited by Martin Stephen
*Anthem for Doomed Youth* edited by Lyn Macdonald

# Contents

# Introduction

Thousands of poems have been written about the First World War. The famous poets are Rupert Brooke, Wilfred Owen, Isaac Rosenburg and Siegfried Sassoon, but many other poets also wrote about this war. So too did many people who would not necessarily have written poetry if the events of 1914 to 1918 had not inspired or horrified them. In an attempt to give a full view of the war I have included poems from all three groups. Some of the pieces are undoubtedly great whilst others would probably not have survived but for the picture they paint, and it was this picture I was after; all aspects of the war described in verse.

The anthology is divided into themes rather than events or dates and begins just before the outbreak of war in 1914. Britain is seen as an idyllic country (at least in the eyes of many poets) and at first the war inspired a feeling of patriotic enthusiasm. This was the first war to be fought extensively on land, sea and in the air and, although the Trench Poets are the most numerous, I have included sections on each of the forces. Eric Simson, a soldier, airman and flying instructor, has never been in print before and many of the air and sea poets are not well known. This was also the first war in which women were involved to any great extent. Some of these women wrote enthusiastically about the war, others about the loss of family, friends or lovers. Many actively participated in the war effort, taking on jobs that had been done by men who were now away fighting.

As well as the various fronts on which the war was fought, it affected those at home. Bombs threatened the towns and, for the first time in history, everyone was involved in the conflict. Country estates, such as Castle Drogo in Devon and Lanhydrock in Cornwall, were left without servants as able-bodied men signed up to fight. Others, such as Stourhead in Wiltshire, lost their heirs. In some cases, such as the Cawleys of Berrington Hall in Herefordshire, almost an entire generation of sons were killed. Rudyard Kipling, like many others, never got over the death of his son Jack and the boy's room at Bateman's was left as it was, awaiting his return. The sudden deaths of so many men, both workers and heirs, was the reason that the National Trust began to take on the great country houses of England, which would otherwise have been lost. Many of the properties, such as Dunham Massey in Cheshire and Clandon Park in Surrey, show vividly what it was like to have been involved in the greatest war man had known. They acted as hospitals, convalescent homes, airfields, intelligence centres, or their land was turned over to intensive food production. The poets abroad, especially those on the ravaged and sodden Western Front, fondly remembered the gentle 'English Air' and fields of home, even though the fields often, in fact, lay fallow and untended as their workers fought at the front.

The Battle of the Somme in 1916 challenged many peoples' preconceived views of the war. Were the huge numbers of casualties justified? Some men were taken prisoner, others deserted or were court martialled for disobedience, while vast numbers died or were permanently injured. Wilfred Owen and Siegfried Sassoon were not the only poets to question whether fighting the war was going to achieve anything. Rev. G. A. Studdert Kennedy, a vicar on the Western Front, questioned the decisions of the politicians and leaders at home and Edward

Thomas challenged the ideals for which he was supposedly fighting.

Amidst the horrors of war, animals were true and loyal allies. Horses, dogs and birds were all used and gave their lives in large numbers to help the cause. Particularly on the Western Front, the peace and beauty of nature stood in sharp contrast to the violence and filth of war. Flowers still grew in the battle fields, sunrises and sunsets still inflamed the skies and each year spring came, bringing with it hope of better times.

The last two sections concern the period after the war. After the Armistice, people tried to rebuild their shattered lives, amidst a prevailing atmosphere of grief and disillusion. The war memorials in every town and village, the tomb of the Unknown Warrior in Westminster Abbey and, I hope, the final chapter of this anthology will ensure that we never forget the sacrifice that so many made.

I have chosen poems by people who experienced the war, directly and indirectly, predominantly from the British Isles. There are exceptions; when I thought a poem was particularly important ('In Flanders Fields') or described a particular event ('Cher Ami'). It was hard to try to present an accurate picture of this appalling conflict in only ninety poems and there are many regrettable omissions. Where possible, I tried to avoid cutting poems and this has led to some exclusions, notably David Jones' 'In Parenthesis', which I feel needs to be read in its entirety.

My hope is that this anthology will describe different facets of the First World War and act as a tribute to A. E. Housman's 'young men' in this commemorative year.

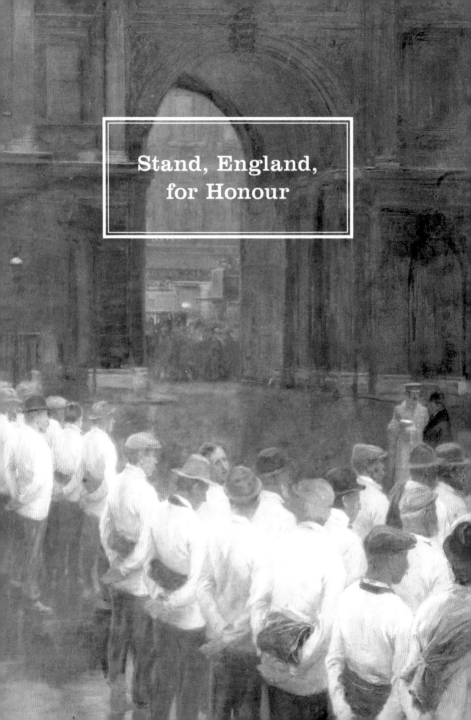

Stand, England,
for Honour

# Wake Up, England

Thou careless, awake!
Thou peace-maker, fight!
Stand, England, for honour,
And God guard the Right!

Thy mirth lay aside,
Thy cavil and play:
The foe is upon thee,
And grave is the day.

The monarch Ambition
Hath harnessed his slaves;
But the folk of the Ocean
Are free as the waves.

For Peace thou art armed
Thy Freedom to hold:
Thy Courage as iron,
Thy Good-faith as gold.

Through Fire, Air and Water
Thy trial must be:
But they that love life best
Die gladly for thee.

The Love of their mothers
Is strong to command:
The fame of their fathers
Is might to their hand.

Much suffering shall cleanse thee:
But thou through the flood
Shalt win to Salvation,
To Beauty through blood.

Up, careless, awake!
Ye peacemakers, Fight!
ENGLAND STANDS FOR HONOUR.
GOD DEFEND THE RIGHT!

**Robert Bridges**
**(1844–1930)**

First published in *The Times* 8 August 1914

# 1914  I: Peace

Now, God be thanked who has matched us with His hour,
  And caught our youth, and wakened us from sleeping,
With hand made sure, clear eye, and sharpened power,
  To turn, as swimmers into cleanness leaping,
Glad from a world grown old and cold and weary,
  Leave the sick hearts that honour could not move,
And half-men, and their dirty songs and dreary,
  And all the little emptiness of love!

Oh! we, who have known shame, we have found release there,
  Where there's no ill, no grief, but sleep has mending,
    Naught broken save this body, lost but breath;
Nothing to shake the laughing heart's long peace there
  But only agony, and that has ending:
    And the worst friend and enemy is but Death.

**Rupert Brooke**
**(1887–1915)**

This is the first poem in Rupert Brooke's sonnet sequence, '1914'.
The poems were written between December 1914 and January 1915.

# Happy is England Now

There is not anything more wonderful
Than a great people moving towards the deep
Of an unguessed and unfeared future; nor
Is aught so dear of all held dear before
As the new passion stirring in their veins
When the destroying Dragon wakes from sleep.

Happy is England now, as never yet!
And though the sorrows of the slow days fret
Her faithfullest children, grief itself is proud.
Ev'n the warm beauty of this spring and summer
That turns to bitterness turns then to gladness
Since for this England the beloved ones died.

Happy is England in the brave that die
For wrongs not hers and wrongs so sternly hers;
Happy in those that give, give, and endure
The pain that never the new years may cure;
Happy in all her dark woods, green fields, towns,
Her hills and rivers and her chafing sea.

What'er was dear before is dearer now.
There's not a bird singing upon his bough
But sings the sweeter in our English ears:
There's not a nobleness of heart, hand, brain
But shines the purer; happiest is England now
In those that fight, and watch with pride and tears.

**John Freeman**
**(1880–1929)**

# Men Who March Away

### (Song of the Soldiers)

What of the faith and fire within us
    Men who march away
    Ere the barn-cocks say
    Night is growing grey,
Leaving all that here can win us;
What of the faith and fire within us
    Men who march away?

Is it a purblind prank, O think you,
    Friend with the musing eye,
    Who watch us stepping by
    With doubt and dolorous sigh?
Can much pondering so hoodwink you!
Is it a purblind prank, O think you,
    Friend with the musing eye?

Nay. We well see what we are doing,
    Though some may not see –
    Dalliers as they be –
    England's need are we;
Her distress would leave us rueing:
Nay. We well see what we are doing,
    Though some may not see!

In our heart of hearts believing
   Victory crowns the just,
   And that braggarts must
   Surely bite the dust,
Press we to the field ungrieving,
In our heart of hearts believing
   Victory crowns the just.

Hence the faith and fire within us
   Men who march away
   Ere the barn-cocks say
   Night is growing grey,
Leaving all that here can win us;
Hence the faith and fire within us
   Men who march away.

**Thomas Hardy**
**(1840–1928)**

Written 5 September 1914
Published in the *TLS* 10 September 1914
and in the *NY Times* 11 September 1914.
The National Trust looks after Hardy's Cottage (his birthplace)
and Max Gate, where he wrote much of his work,
particularly his poetry.

# The Call

Ah! we have dwelt in Arcady long time
    With sun and youth eternal round our ways
And in the magic of that golden clime
    We loved the pageant of the passing days.

The wonderful white dawns of frost and flame
    In winter, and the swift sun's upward leap;
Or summer's stealthy wakening that came
    Soft as a whisper on the lips of sleep.

And there were woodland hollows of green lawn,
    Where boys with windy hair and wine wet lips
Danced on the sunsplashed grass; and the hills of dawn
    That looked out seaward to the distant ships.

In infinite still night the moon swam low
    And saffron in a silver dusted sky;
Beauty and sorrow hand in hand with slow
    Soft wings and soundless passage wandered by.

And white roads vanishing beneath the sky
    Called for our feet, and there were countless things
That we must see and do, while blood was high
    And time still hovered on reluctant wings.

And these were good; yet in our heart we knew
  These were not all, – that still through toil and pains
Deeds of a purer lustre given to few,
  Made for the perfect glory that remains.

And when the summons in our ears was shrill
  Unshaken in our trust we rose, and then
Flung but a backward glance, and care-free still
  Went strongly forth to do the work of men.

**W. N. Hodgson**
**(1893–1916)**

# The Recruit
## from: A Shropshire Lad

Leave your home behind, lad,
    And reach your friends your hand,
And go, and luck go with you
    While Ludlow tower shall stand.

Oh, come you home of Sunday
    When Ludlow streets are still
And Ludlow bells are calling
    To farm and lane and mill,

Or come you home of Monday
    When Ludlow market hums
And Ludlow chimes are playing
    'The conquering hero comes',

Come you home a hero
    Or come not home at all,
The lads you leave will mind you
    Till Ludlow tower shall fall.

And you will list the bugle
    That blows in lands of morn,
And make the foes of England
    Be sorry you were born.

And you till trump of doomsday
    On lands of morn may lie,
And make the hearts of comrades
    Be heavy where you die.

Leave your home behind you,
    Your friends by field and town:
Oh, town and field will mind you
    Till Ludlow tower is down.

**A. E. Housman**
**(1859–1936)**

# "For All We Have and Are"
### 1914

For all we have and are,
For all our children's fate,
Stand up and take the war,
The Hun is at the gate!
Our world has passed away,
In wantonness o'erthrown.
There is nothing left to-day
But steel and fire and stone!
    Though all we knew depart,
    The old Commandments stand:-
    "In courage keep your heart,
    In strength lift up your hand."

Once more we hear the word
That sickened earth of old:-
"No law except the Sword
Unsheathed and uncontrolled."
Once more it knits mankind,
Once more the nations go
To meet and break and bind
A crazed and driven foe.

Comfort, content, delight,
The ages' slow-bought gain,
They shrivelled in a night.
Only ourselves remain
To face the naked days
In silent fortitude,
Through perils and dismays
Renewed and re-renewed.
> Though all we made depart,
> The old Commandments stand:-
> "In patience keep your heart,
> In strength lift up you hand."

No easy hope or lies
Shall bring us to our goal,
But iron sacrifice
Of body, will, and soul.
There is but one task for all –
One life for each to give.
Who stands if Freedom fall?
Who dies if England live?

**Rudyard Kipling**
**(1865–1936)**

# English Fields

### from: August, 1914

How still this quiet cornfield is to-night!
By an intenser glow the evening falls,
Bringing, not darkness, but a deeper light;
Among the stooks a partridge covey calls.

The windows glitter on the distant hill;
Beyond the hedge the sheep-bells in the fold
Stumble on sodden music and are still;
The forlorn pinewoods droop above the wold.

An endless quiet valley reaches out
Past the blue hills into the evening sky;
Over the stubble, cawing, goes a rout
Of rooks from harvest, flagging as they fly.

So beautiful it is, I never saw
So great a beauty on these English fields
Touched by the twilight's coming into awe,
Ripe to the soul and rich with summer's yields.

**John Masefield**
**(1878–1967)**

# Summer in England, 1914

On London fell a clearer light;
    Caressing pencils of the sun
Defined the distances, the white
    Houses transfigured one by one,
The 'long, unlovely street' impearled.
O what a sky has walked the world!

Most happy year! And out of town
    The hay was prosperous, and the wheat;
The silken harvest climbed the down:
    Moon after moon was heavenly-sweet,
Stroking the bread within the sheaves,
Looking 'twixt apples and their leaves.

And while this rose made round her cup,
    The armies died convulsed. And when
This chaste young silver sun went up
    Softly, a thousand shattered men,
One wet corruption heaped the plain,
After a league-long throb of pain.

Flower following tender flower; and birds,
    And berries; and benignant skies
Made thrive the serried flocks and herds. –
    Yonder are men shot through the eyes.
    Love, hide thy face
From man's unpardonable race.

Who said 'No man hath greater love than this,
     To die to serve his friend'?
So these have loved us all unto the end.
     Chide thou no more, O thou unsacrificed!
The soldier dying dies upon a kiss,
     The very kiss of Christ.

**Alice Meynell**
**(1847–1922)**

# All the Hills and Vales Along

All the hills and vales along
Earth is bursting into song,
And the singers are the chaps
Who are going to die perhaps.
    O sing, marching men,
    Till the valleys ring again.
    Give your gladness to earth's keeping,
    So be glad, when you are sleeping.

Cast away regret and rue,
Think what you are marching to.
Little live, great pass.
Jesus Christ and Barabbas
Were found the same day.
This died, that went his way.
    So sing with joyful breath,
    For why, you are going to death.
    Teeming earth will surely store
    All the gladness that you pour.

Earth that never doubts nor fears,
Earth that knows of death, not tears,
Earth that bore with joyful ease
Hemlock for Socrates,
Earth that blossomed and was glad
'Neath the cross that Christ had,

Shall rejoice and blossom too
When the bullet reaches you.
    Wherefore, men marching
    On the road to death, sing!
    Pour gladness on earth's head,
    So be merry, so be dead.

From the hills and valleys earth
Shouts back the sound of mirth,
Tramp of feet and lilt of song
Ringing all the roads along.
All the music of their going,
Ringing swinging glad song-throwing,
Earth will echo still, when foot
Lies numb and voice mute.
    On, marching men, on
    To the gates of death with song
    Sow your gladness for earth's reaping,
    So you may be glad, though sleeping.
    Strew your gladness on earth's bed,
    So be merry, so be dead.

**Charles Hamilton Sorley**
**(1895–1915)**

The Torn Earth

# The Soldier's Cigarette

## (October 1915)

I'm cheap and insignificant,
    I'm easy quite to get,
In every place I show my face
    They call me cigarette.

They buy me four a penny, throw
    Me down without regret,
The elegant, the nonchalant,
    The blasé cigarette.

I'm small and nothing much to see,
    But men won't soon forget
How unafraid my part I've played,
    The dauntless cigarette.

When trenches all are water-logged
    I'm thereabouts, you bet,
With cheery smile the hours I while,
    The patient cigarette.

I sit within the trenches and
    Upon the parapet
Jack Johnson's shock with scorn I mock,
    The careless cigarette.

If bullets whizz and Bill gets hit,
    Don't hurry for the 'vet.',
It's 'I'm alright, give us a light,'
    And 'Where's my cigarette?'

Ubiquitous and agile too,
    I'm but a youngster yet,
The debonair, the savoir faire
    Abandoned cigarette.

When meals are few and far between,
    When spirit's ebb has set,
When comrades fall, and Death's gates call,
    Who's there but cigarette?

I cool the mind and quiet the brain
    When danger's to be met;
When more is vain I ease the pain,
    Immortal cigarette!

**Harold Beckh**
**(1894–1916)**

# The Zonnebeke Road

Morning, if this late withered light can claim
Some kindred with that merry flame
Which the young day was wont to fling through space!
Agony stares from each grey face.
And yet the day is come; stand down! stand down!
Your hands unclasp from rifles while you can,
The frost has pierced them to the bended bone?
Why, see old Stevens there, that iron man,
Melting the ice to shave his grotesque chin:
Go ask him, shall we win?
I never liked this bay, some foolish fear
Caught me the first time that I came in here;
That dugout fallen in awakes, perhaps,
Some formless haunting of some corpse's chaps.
True, and wherever we have held the line,
There were such corners, seeming-saturnine
For no good cause. Now where Haymarket starts,
That is no place for soldiers with weak hearts;
The minenwerfers have it to the inch.
Look, how the snow-dust whisks along the road,
Piteous and silly; the stones themselves must flinch
In this east wind; the low sky like a load
Hangs over – a dead weight. But what a pain

Must gnaw where its clay cheek
Crushes the shell-chopped trees that fang the plain –
The ice-bound throat gulps out a gargoyle shriek.
The wretched wire before the village line
Rattles like rusty brambles or dead bine,
And then the daylight oozes into dun;
Black pillars, those are trees where roadways run.
Even Ypres now would warm our souls; fond fool,
Our tour's but one night old, seven more to cool!
O screaming dumbness, O dull clashing death,
Shreds of dead grass and willows, homes and men,
Watch as you will, men clench their chattering teeth
And freeze you back with that one hope, disdain.

**Edmund Blunden**
**(1896–1974)**

This poem was written during the Third Battle of Ypres, 1917.

# From the Somme

In other days I sang of simple things,
    Of summer dawn, and summer noon and night,
The dewy grass, the dew-wet fairy rings,
    The lark's long golden flight.

Deep in the forest I made melody
    While squirrels cracked their hazel nuts on high,
Or I would cross the wet sand to the sea
    And sing to sea and sky.

When came the silvered silence of the night
    I stole to casements over scented lawns,
And softly sang of love and love's delight
    To mute white marble fauns.

Oft in the tavern parlour I would sing
    Of morning sun upon the morning vine,
And, calling for a chorus, sweep the string
    In praise of good red wine.

I played with all the toys the gods provide,
    I sang my songs and made glad holiday.
Now I have cast my broken toys aside
    And flung my lute away.

A singer once, I now am fain to weep.
    Within my soul I feel strange music swell,
Vast chants of tragedy too deep – too deep
    For my poor lips to tell.

**Leslie Coulson**
**(1889–j1916)**

# Chemin Des Dames

In silks and satins the ladies went
Where the breezes sighed and the poplars bent,
Taking the air of a Sunday morn
Midst the red of poppies and gold of corn –
Flowery ladies in stiff brocades,
With negro pages and serving-maids,
In scarlet coach or in gilt sedan,
With brooch and buckle and flounce and fan,
Patch and powder and trailing scent,
Under the trees the ladies went –
Lovely ladies that gleamed and glowed,
As they took their air on the Ladies' Road.

Boom of thunder and lightning flash –
The torn earth rocks to the barrage crash;
The bullets whine and the bullets sing
From the mad machine-guns chattering;
Black smoke rolling across the mud,
Trenches plastered with flesh and blood –
The blue ranks lock with the ranks of grey,
Stab and swagger and sob and sway;
The living cringe from the shrapnel bursts,
The dying moan of their burning thirsts,
Moan and die in the gulping slough –
Where are the butterfly ladies now?

**Crosbie Garstin**
**(1887–1930)**

Crosbie Garstin fought on the Western Front and wrote this
while in the trenches, waiting to go into action.

# The Silent One

Who died on the wires, and hung there, one of two –
Who for his hours of life had chattered through
Infinite lovely chatter of Bucks accent:
Yet faced unbroken wires; stepped over, and went
A noble fool, faithful to his stripes – and ended.
But I weak, hungry, and willing only for the chance
Of line – to fight in the line, lay down under unbroken
Wires, and saw the flashes, and kept unshaken,
Till the politest voice – a finicking accent, said:
'Do you think you might crawl through, there; there's a hole'
Darkness, shot at: I smiled, as politely replied –
'I'm afraid not, Sir.' There was no hole no way to be seen
Nothing but chance of death, after tearing of clothes.
Kept flat, and watched the darkness, hearing bullets whizzing –
And thought of music – and swore deep heart's deep oaths
(Polite to God) and retreated and came on again,
Again retreated – and a second time faced the screen.

**Ivor Gurney**
**(1890–1937)**

39

# A Carol from Flanders

In Flanders on the Christmas morn
The trenched foemen lay,
The German and the Briton born,
And it was Christmas day.

The red sun rose on fields accurst,
The grey fog fled away;
But neither cared to fire the first,
For it was Christmas Day!

They called from each to each across
The hideous disarray,
For terrible had been their loss:
'Oh, this is Christmas Day!'

Their rifles all they set aside,
One impulse to obey;
'Twas just the men on either side,
Just men – and Christmas day.

They dug the graves for all their dead
And over them did pray:
And Englishmen and Germans said:
'How strange a Christmas Day!'

Between the trenches then they met,
Shook hands and e'en did play
At games on which their hearts were set
On happy Christmas Day.

Not all the emperors and kings,
Financiers and they
Who rule us could prevent these things –
For it was Christmas Day.

Oh ye who read this truthful rime
From Flanders, kneel and say:
God speed the time when every day
Shall be as Christmas Day.

**Frederick Niven**
**(1878–1944)**

On Christmas Day, 1914, the troops on both sides of the
Western Front left their trenches and walked into no-man's-land.
There they celebrated as best they could, exchanged gifts,
played football and buried their dead. The following day war resumed.

# Dulce Et Decorum Est

Bent double, like old beggars under sacks,
Knock-kneed, coughing like hags, we cursed through sludge,
Till on the haunting flares we turned our backs
And towards our distant rest began to trudge.
Men marched asleep. Many had lost their boots
But limped on, blood-shod. All went lame; all blind;
Drunk with fatigue; deaf even to the hoots
Of tired, outstripped Five-Nines that dropped behind.

Gas! Gas! Quick, boys! – An ecstasy of fumbling,
Fitting the clumsy helmets just in time;
But someone still was yelling out and stumbling
And flound'ring like a man in fire or lime. . .
Dim, through the misty panes and thick green light,
As under a green sea, I saw him drowning.

In all my dreams, before my helpless sight,
He plunges at me, guttering, choking, drowning.

If in some smothering dreams you too could pace
Behind the wagon that we flung him in,
And watch the white eyes writhing in his face,
His hanging face, like a devil's sick of sin;
If you could hear, at every jolt, the blood
Come gargling from the froth-corrupted lungs,
Obscene as cancer, bitter as the cud
Of vile, incurable sores on innocent tongues,
My friend, you would not tell us with such high zest
To children ardent for some desperate glory,
The old Lie: Dulce et decorum est
Pro patria mori.

**Wilfred Owen**
**(1893–1918)**

Early drafts were headed 'To Jessie Pope etc.' or 'To a certain Poetess.'

# The Nut's Birthday

When Gilbert's birthday came *last* spring,
    Oh! how our brains we racked
To try and find a single thing
    Our languid dear one lacked;
For, since he nestled at his ease
    Upon the lap of Plenty,
Stock birthday presents failed to please
    The Nut of two and twenty.

And so we bought, to suit his taste –
    Refined and dilettante –
Some ormolu, grotesquely chased;
    A little bronze Bacchante;
A flagon of the Stuarts' reign;
    A 'Corot' to content him.
Well, now his birthday's come again,
    And *this* is what we sent him:

Some candles and a bar of soap,
    Cakes, peppermints and matches,
A pot of jam, some thread (like rope)
    For stitching khaki patches.
These gifts, our soldier writes to say,
    Have brought him untold riches
To celebrate his natal day
    In hard-won Flanders' ditches.

**Jessie Pope**
**(1868–1941)**

# The Immortals

I killed them, but they would not die.
Yea! all the day and all the night
For them I could not rest nor sleep,
Nor guard from them nor hide in flight.

Then in my agony I turned
And made my hands red in their gore.
In vain – for faster than I slew
They rose more cruel than before.

I killed and killed with slaughter mad;
I killed till all my strength was gone.
And still they rose to torture me,
For Devils only die in fun.

I used to think the Devil hid
In women's smiles and wine's carouse.
I called him Satan, Balzebub.
But now I call him, dirty louse.

**Isaac Rosenberg**
**(1890–1918)**

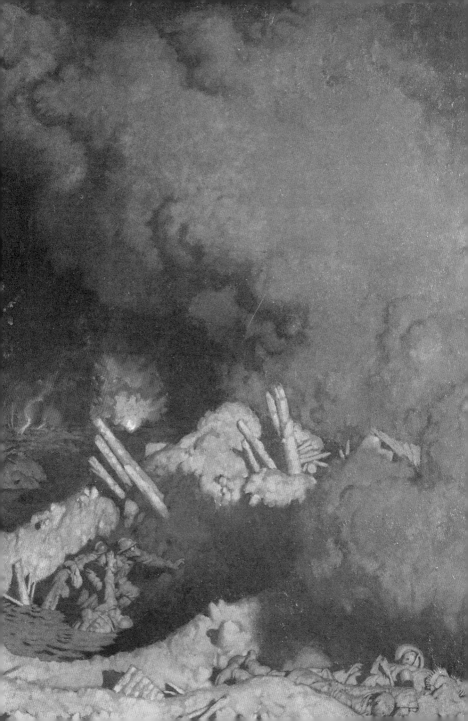

# Attack

At dawn the ridge emerges massed and dun
In the wild purple of the glow'ring sun
Smouldering through spouts of drifting smoke that shroud
The menacing scarred slope; and, one by one,
Tanks creep and topple forward to the wire.
The barrage roars and lifts. Then, clumsily bowed
With bombs and guns and shovels and battle-gear,
Men jostle and climb to meet the bristling fire.
Lines of grey, muttering faces, masked with fear,
They leave their trenches, going over the top,
While time ticks blank and busy on their wrists,
And hope, with furtive eyes and grappling fists,
Flounders in mud. O Jesus, make it stop!

**Siegfried Sassoon**
**(1886–1967)**

# Fricourt

I sleep in a hut in Fricourt Wood
    With an eight inch dud beside me;
And the stricken trees hold stiff in the breeze
    Gaunt arms that seem to deride me.
And out of the mist I hear a voice,
    As I lie asleep and dreaming,
Ye may sleep in peace on your bed of fleece
    And never a shell flies screaming;
For the day is past when the air was rent
    With the shells and shrieks of the dying,
When the sun shone red on many a head
    That in Fricourt Wood was lying.

There were men from the North and the East and West,
    Where the setting sun goes down;
There were men whose fame was a household name,
    There were men of no renown.
There were old and young and middle-aged,
    From the plough as well as the city;
But they chased as a man when the fight began,
    And they asked and gave no pity;
When the foremost fell, they still came on,
    They were thinned but never shaken;
But the blood of the true lay as thick as the dew
    When Fricourt Wood was taken.

They sleep in the earth in Fricourt Wood,
     With a foot of soil above them;
And in far off lands there are weary hands,
     And broken hearts that loved them.
And though there shall come a golden crop,
     'Tis other hands shall reap it –
Still they fought for the Wood and they gained the Wood,
     Their's is the Wood and they keep it.
And the moon looks down on the pile of chalk
     Where the little chateau stood,
And the mist is pale like a silver veil
     And there's peace in Fricourt Wood.

**Eric Simson**
**(1895–1956)**

Written at Longueval, October 1916

# The Night Patrol

Over the top! The wire's thin here, unbarbed
Plain rusty coils, not staked, and low enough:
Full of old tins, though – 'When you're through, all three,
Aim quarter left for fifty yards or so,
Then straight for that new piece of German wire;
See if it's thick, and listen for a while
For sound of working; don't run any risks;
About an hour; now over!' And we placed
Our hands on the topmost sand-bags, leapt, and stood
A second with curved backs, then crept to the wire,
Wormed ourselves tinkling through, glanced back, and dropped.
The sodden ground was splashed with shallow pools,
And tufts of crackling cornstalks, now two years old,
No man had reaped, and patches of spring grass,
Half-seen, as rose and sank the flares, were strewn
With the wrecks of our attack: the bandoliers,
Packs, rifles, bayonets, belts, and haversacks,
Shell fragments, and the huge whole forms of shells
Shot fruitlessly – and everywhere the dead.
Only the dead were always present – present
As a vile sickly smell of rottenness;
The rustling stubble and the early grass,
The slimy pools – the dead men stank through all,
Pungent and sharp; as bodies loomed before,
And as we passed, they stank; then dulled away
To that vague factor, all encompassing,
Infecting earth and air. They lay, all  clothed,

Each in some new and piteous attitude
That we well marked to guide us back; as he,
Outside our wire, that lay on his back and crossed
His legs Crusader-wise; I smiled at that,
And thought of Elia and his Temple Church.
From him, a quarter left, lay a small corpse,
Down in a hollow, huddled as in bed,
That one of us put his hand on unawares.
Next was a bunch of half a dozen men
All blown to bits, an archipelago
Of corrupt fragments, vexing us to three,
Who had no light to see by, save the flares.
On such a trail, so lit, for ninety yards
We crawled on belly and elbows, till we saw,
Instead of lumpish dead before our eyes,
The stakes and crosslines of the German wire.
We lay in shelter of the last dead man,
Ourselves as dead, and heard their shovels ring
Turning the earth, their talk and cough at times.
A sentry fired and a machine-gun spat;
They shot a flare above us, when it fell
And spluttered out in the pools of No Man's Land,
We turned and crawled past the remembered dead:
Past him and him, and them and him, until,
For he lay some way apart, we caught the scent
Of the Crusader and slid past his legs,
And through the wire and home, and got our rum.

**Arthur Graeme West**
**(1891–1917)**

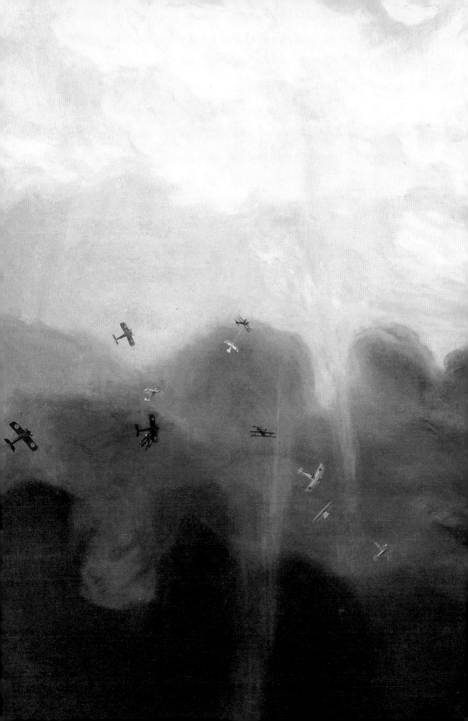

of Steel

# A Poor Aviator Lay Dying

Oh, a poor aviator lay dying
At the end of a bright summer's day,
His comrades were gathered around him
To carry the fragments away.

The engine was piled on his wishbone,
The Hotchkiss was wrapped round his head,
A spark-plug stuck out at each elbow
It was plain that he'd shortly be dead.

He spat out a valve and a gasket
And stirred in the sump where he lay,
And then to his wond'ring comrades,
These brave parting words he did say;

'Take the manifold out of my larynx
And the butterfly valve off my neck
Remove from my kidneys the camrods
There's a lot of good parts in this wreck.

'Take the piston rings out of my stomach,
And the cylinders out of my brain,
Extract from my liver the crankshaft,
And assemble the engine again.

'I'll be riding a cloud in the morning
With no rotary before me to cuss,
So shake the lead from your feet and get busy,
There's another lad wanting this 'bus.'

**Anon**

# The Dawn Patrol

Sometimes I fly at dawn above the sea,
Where, underneath, the restless waters flow –
    Silver, and cold, and slow.
Dim in the east there burns a new-born sun,
Where rosy gleams along the ripples run,
    Save where the mist droops low,
Hiding the level loneliness from me.

And now appears beneath the milk-white haze
A little fleet of anchored ships, which lie
    In clustered company,
And seem as they are yet fast bound by sleep,
Although the day has long begun to peep,
    With red-inflamèd eye,
Along the still, deserted ocean ways.

The fresh, cold wind of dawn blows on my face
As in the sun's raw heart I swiftly fly,
    And watch the seas glide by.
Scarce human seem I, moving through the skies,
And far removed from warlike enterprise –
    Like some great gull on high
Whose white and gleaming wings bear on through space.

Then do I feel with God quite, quite alone,
High in the virgin morn, so white and still,
    And free from human ill:
My prayers transcend my feeble earth-bound plaints –
As though I sang among the happy Saints
    With many a holy thrill –
As though the glowing sun were God's bright Throne.

My flight is done. I cross the line of foam
That breaks around a town of grey and red,
    Whose streets and squares lie dead
Beneath the silent dawn – then I am proud
That England's peace to guard I am allowed;
    Then bow my humble head,
In thanks to Him Who brings me safely home.

**Paul Bewsher**
**(1894–1966)**

# The Zeppelin

Guns! far and near,
Quick, sudden, angry,
They startle the still street
Upturned faces appear,
Doors open on darkness,
There is a hurrying of feet,

And whirled athwart the gloom
White fingers of alarm
Point at last there
Where illumined and dumb
A shape suspended
Hovers, a demon of the starry air!

Strange and cold as a dream
Of sinister fancy,
It charms like a snake,
Poised deadly in a gleam,
While bright explosions
Leap up to it and break.

Is it terror you seek
To exult in? Know then
Hearts are here
That the plunging beak
Of night-winged havoc
Strikes not with fear

So much as it stings
To a deep elation
And a quivering pride
That at last the hour brings
For them too the danger
Of those who died,

Of those who yet fight,
Spending for each of us
Their glorious blood
In the foreign night, –
That now we are neared to them
Thank we God.

**Laurence Binyon**
**(1869–1943)**

# The Birds of Steel

This apple tree, that once was green,
    Is now a thousand flowers in one!
And, with their bags strapped to their thighs,
    There's many a bee that comes for sweets,
To stretch each bag to its full size.

And when the night has grown a moon,
    And I lie half-asleep in bed,
I hear those bees again – ah no,
    It is the birds of steel instead,
Seeking their innocent prey below.

Man-ridden birds of steel, unseen,
    That come to drop their murdering lime
On any child or harmless thing
    Before the early morning time:
Up, nearer to God, they fly and sing.

**W. H. Davies**
**(1871–1940)**

# Dawn

'Machines will raid at dawn,' they say:
It's always dawn, or just before;
why choose this wretched time of day
    for making war?

From all the hours of light there are
why do they always choose the first?
Is it because they know it's far
    and far the worst?

Is it a morbid sense of fun
that makes them send us day by day
a target for the sportive Hun? –
    who knows our way,

and waits for us at dawn's first peep,
knowing full well we shall be there,
and he, when that is done, may sleep
    without a care.

And was it not Napoleon
who said (in French) these words, 'Lor' lumme!
no man can hope to fight upon
    an empty tummy'?

Yet every morn we bold bird-boys
clamber into our little buses,
and go and make a futile noise
    with bombs and cusses.

And every night the orders tell
the same monotonous story
'machines will raid at dawn.' To hell
    with death or glory!

Why can't they let us lie in bed
and, after breakfast and a wash,
despatch us, clean and fully fed,
    to kill the Boche?

I hate the dawn, as dogs hate soap:
and on my heart, when I am done,
you'll find the words engraved, 'Dawn hope-
    less, streak of, one.

**Jeffrey Day**
**(1896–1918)**

# Height

Save for the rush of wind against my face
    All sense of speed is lost;
I hang suspended motionless in space,
While ice draws down on the planes a feathery trace
    Shed by the aetherial frost.

So far below our glorious earth is seen,
    Immeasurably remote;
Diverging lines with blotches in between,
Just like a pattern that has lost its sheen
    Upon a threadbare coat

I shudder neath the passionless caress
    Of this unearthly cold;
All the while the utter loneliness
Weighs on my mind, nor can I yet suppress
    Its terrifying hold.

**Eric Simson**
**(1895–1956)**

# An Irish Airman Forsees His Death

I know that I shall meet my fate
Somewhere among the clouds above;
Those that I fight I do not hate,
Those that I guard I do not love;
My country is Kiltartan Cross
My countrymen Kiltartan's poor,
No likely end could bring them loss
Or leave them happier than before.
Nor law, nor duty bade me fight,
Nor public men, nor cheering crowds,
A lonely impulse of delight
Drove to this tumult in the clouds;
I balanced all, brought all to mind,
The years to come seemed waste of breath,
A waste of breath the years behind
In balance with this life, this death.

**W. B. Yeats**
**(1865–1939)**

# Action Stations
# Fore and Aft

# North Sea

Dawn on the drab North Sea! –
colourless, cold, and depressing,
with the sun that we long to see
refraining from his blessing.
To the westward – sombre as doom:
to the eastward – grey and foreboding:
Comes a low, vibrating boom –
the sound of  a mine exploding.

Day on the drear North Sea! –
wearisome, drab, and relentless.
The low clouds swiftly flee;
bitter the sky and relentless.
Nothing at all in sight
save the mast of a sunken trawler,
fighting her long, last fight
with the waves that mouth and maul her.

Gale on the bleak North Sea! –
howling a dirge in the rigging.
Slowly and toilfully
through the great, grey breakers digging,
thus we make our way,
hungry, wet, and weary,
soaked with the sleet and spray,
desolate, damp, and dreary.

Fog in the dank North Sea! –
silent and clammily dripping.
Slowly and mournfully,
ghostlike, goes the shipping.

Sudden across the swell
come the fog-horns hoarsely blaring
or the clang of a warning-bell,
to leave us vainly staring.

Night on the black North Sea! –
black as hell's darkest hollow.
Peering anxiously,
we search for the ships that follow.
One are the sea and sky,
dim are the figures near us,
with only the sea-bird's cry
and the swish of the waves to cheer us.

Death on the wild North Sea! –
death from the shell that shatters
(death we will face with glee,
'tis the weary wait that matters): -
death from the guns that roar,
and the splinters weirdly shrieking.
'Tis a fight to the death; 'tis war;
and the North Sea is redly reeking!

**Jeffrey Day**
**(1896–1918)**

# Destroyers

Through the dark night
And the fury of battle
Pass the destroyers in a shower of spray.
As the Wolf-pack to the flank of cattle,
We shall close in on them – shadows of grey.
In from ahead,
Through shell-flashes red,
We shall come down to them, after the Day.
Whistle and crash
Of salvo and volley
Round us and into us while we attack.
Light on our target they'll flash in their folly,
Splitting our ears with the shrapnel-crack.
Fire as they will,
We'll come to them still,
Roar as they may at us – Back – Go Back!
White through the sea
To the shell-splashes foaming,
We shall be there at the death of the Hun.
Only we pray for a star in the gloaming
(Light for torpedoes and none for a gun).
Lord – of Thy Grace
Make it a race,
Over the sea with the night to run.

**'Klaxon'**
**John Graham Bower**
**(1886–1940)**

# Submarines

When the breaking wavelets pass all sparkling to the sky,
When beyond their crests we see the slender masts go by,
When the glimpses alternate in bubbles white and green,
And funnels grey against the sky show clear and fair between,
When the word is passed along – 'Stern and beam and bow' –
'Action stations fore and aft – all torpedoes now!'
When the hissing tubes are still, as if with bated breath
They waited for the word to loose the silver bolts of death,
When the Watch beneath the Sea shall crown the great Desire,
And hear the coughing rush of air that greets the word to fire,
We'll ask no advantage, Lord – but only would we pray
That they may meet this boat of ours upon their outward way.

'Klaxon'
John Graham Bower
(1886–1940)

# The Search-Lights

### extract: verses 1–3

Shadow for shadow, stripped for fight,
   The lean black cruisers search the sea.
Night-long their level shafts of light
   Revolve, and find no enemy.
Only they know each leaping wave
May hide the lightning, and their grave.

And in the land they guard so well
   Is there no silent watch to keep?
An age is dying, and the bell
   Rings midnight on a vaster deep.
But over all its waves, once more,
The search-lights move, from shore to shore.

And captains that we thought were dead,
   And dreamers that we thought were dumb,
And voices that we thought were fled,
   Arise, and call us, and we come;
And 'Search in thine own soul', they cry;
'For there, too, lurks thine enemy'.

**Alfred Noyes**
**(1880–1958)**

# The Troop Ship

Grotesque and queerly huddled
Contortionists to twist
The sleepy soul to a sleep,
We lie all sorts of ways
And cannot sleep.
The wet wind is so cold,
And the lurching men so careless,
That, should you drop to a doze,
Winds' fumble or men's feet
Are on your face.

**Isaac Rosenberg**
**(1890–1918)**

In May 1916 embarked for France from Southampton

# Mine-sweeping Trawlers

Not ours the fighter's glow,
　　the glory, and the praise.
Unnoticed to and fro
　　we pass our dangerous ways.

We sift the drifting sea,
　　and blindly grope beneath;
obscure and toilsome, we
　　the fishermen of death.

But when the great ships go
　　to battle through the gloom,
our hearts beat high to know
　　we cleared their path of doom.

**Edward Hilton Young**
**(1879–1960)**

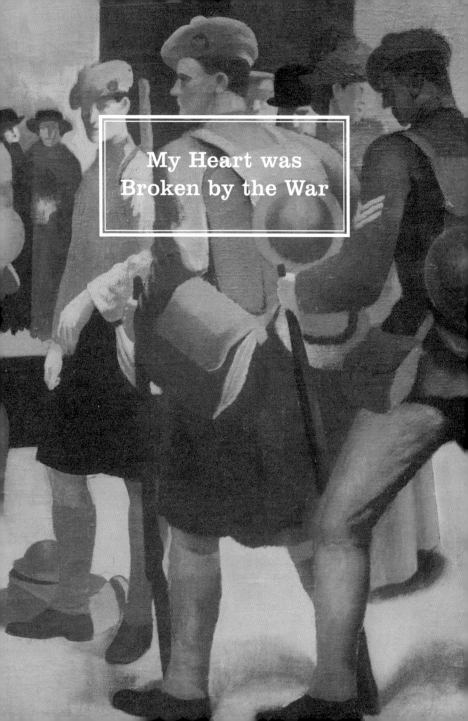

My Heart was
Broken by the War

# To Women

Your hearts are lifted up, your hearts
That have foreknown the utter price.
Your hearts burn upward like a flame
Of splendour and of sacrifice.

For you, you too, to battle go,
Not with the marching drums and cheers
But in the watch of solitude
And through the boundless night of fears.

Swift, swifter than those hawks of war,
Those threatening wings that pulse the air,
Far as the vanward ranks are set,
You are gone before them, you are there!

And not a shot comes blind with death
And not a stab of steel is pressed
Home, but invisibly it tore
And entered first a woman's breast.

Amid the thunder of the guns,
The lightnings of the lance and sword
Your hope, your dread, your throbbing pride,
Your infinite passion is outpoured

From hearts that are as one high heart
Withholding naught from doom and bale
Burningly offered up, – to bleed,
To bear, to break, but not to fail!

**Laurence Binyon**
**(1869–1943)**

# Lamplight

We planned to shake the world together, you and I
Being young, and very wise;
Now in the light of the green shaded lamp
Almost I see your eyes
Light with the old gay laughter; you and I
Dreamed greatly of an Empire in those days,
Setting our feet upon laborious ways,
And all you asked of fame
Was crossed swords in the Army List,
My Dear, against your name.

We planned a great Empire together, you and I,
Bound only by the sea;
Now in the quiet of a chill Winter's night
Your voice comes hushed to me
Full of forgotten memories: you and I
Dreamed great dreams of our future in those days,
Setting our feet on undiscovered ways,
And all I asked of fame
A scarlet cross on my breast, my Dear,
For the swords by your name.

We shall never shake the world together, you and I,
For you gave your life away;
And I think my heart was broken by the war,
Since on a summer day
You took the road we never spoke of: you and I
Dreamed greatly of an Empire in those Days
You set your feet upon the Western ways
And have no need of fame –
There's a scarlet cross on my breast, my Dear,
And a torn cross with your name.

**May Wedderburn Cannan**
**(1893–1973)**

The Army List is the official list of commissioned serving officers in the British Army. Crossed swords indicated that the soldier had been killed or wounded in action.

# Many Sisters to Many Brothers

When we fought campaigns (in the long Christmas rains)
    With soldiers spread in troops on the floor,
I shot as straight as you, my losses were as few,
    My victories as many, or more.
And when in naval battle, amid cannon's rattle,
    Fleet met fleet in the bath,
My cruisers were as trim, my battleships as grim,
    My submarines cut as swift a path.
Or, when it rained too long, and the strength of the strong
    Surged up and broke a way with blows,
I was as fit and keen, my fists hit as clean,
    Your black eye matched my bleeding nose.
Was there a scrap or ploy in which you, the boy,
    Could better me? You could not climb higher,
Ride straighter, run as quick (and to smoke made you sick)
    … But I sit here, and you're under fire.

Oh, it's you that have the luck, out there in the blood and muck:
    You were born beneath a kindly star;
All we dreamt, I and you, you can really go and do,
    And I can't, the way things are.
In a trench you are sitting, while I am knitting
    A hopeless sock that never gets done.
Well, here's luck, my dear – and you've got it, no fear;
    But for me … a war is poor fun.

**Rose Macaulay**
**(1881–1958)**

# War Girls

There's the girl who clips your ticket for the train,
    And the girl who speeds the lift from floor to floor,
There's the girl who does the milk-round in the rain,
    And the girl who calls for orders at your door.
        Strong, sensible and fit,
        They're out to show their grit,
    And tackle jobs with energy and knack.
        No longer caged and penned up,
        They're gong to keep their end up
Till the khaki soldier boys come marching back.

There's the motor girl who drives a heavy van,
    There's the butcher girl who brings your joint of meat,
There's the girl who cries 'All fares, please!' like a man,
    And the girl who whistles taxis up the street.
        Beneath each uniform
        Beats a heart that's soft and warm,
    Though of canny mother-wit they show no lack;
        But a solemn statement this is,
        They've no time for love and kisses
Till the khaki soldier boys come marching back.

**Jessie Pope**
**(1868–1941)**

# Moonrise Over Battlefield

After the fallen sun the wind was sad
like violins behind immense old walls.
Trees were musicians swaying round the bed
of a woman in gloomy halls.

In the privacy of music she made ready
with comb and silver dust and fard;
under her silken vest her little belly
shone like a bladder of sweet lard.

She drifted with the grand air of a punk
on Heaven's streets soliciting white saints;
then lay in bright communion on a cloud-bank
as one who near extreme of pleasure faints.

Then I thought, standing in the ruined trench,
(all around, dead Boche white-shirted slumped
   like sheep),
'Why does this damned entrancing bitch
choose all her lovers among them that sleep?'

**Edgell Rickword**
**(1898–1982)**

# To C. H. V.

What shall I bring to you, wife of mine?
When I come back from the war?
A ribbon your dear brown hair to twine?
A shawl from a Berlin store?
Say, should I choose you some Prussian hack
When the Uhlans we o'erwhelm?
Shall I bring you a Potsdam goblet back
And the crest from a Prince's helm?

Little you'd care what I laid at your feet.
Ribbon or crest or shawl –
What if I bring you nothing, sweet,
Nor maybe come home at all?
Ah, but you'll know, Brave Heart, you'll know
Two things I'll have kept to send:
Mine honour for which you bade me go
And my love – my love to the end.

**Robert Ernest Vernède**
**(1875–1917)**

# An English Air

# When I Come Home

When I come home, dear folk o'mine,
We'll drink a cup of olden wine;
And yet, however rich it be,
No wine will taste so good to me
As English air. How I shall thrill
To drink it in on Hampstead Hill
    When I come home!

When I come home, and leave behind
Dark things I would not call to mind,
I'll taste good ale and home-made bread,
And see white sheets and pillows spread.
And there is one who'll softly creep
To kiss me ere I fall asleep,
And tuck me 'neath the counterpane,
And I shall be a boy again,
    When I come home!

When I come home from dark to light,
And tread the roadways long and white,
And tramp the lanes I tramped of yore,
And see the village greens once more,
The tranquil farms, the meadows free,
The friendly trees that nod to me,
And hear the lark beneath the sun,
'Twill be good pay for what I've done,
    When I come home!

**Lesley Coulson**
**(1889–1916)**

# Bombardment

The Town has opened to the sun.
Like a flat red lily with a million petals
She unfolds, she comes undone.

A sharp sky brushes upon
The myriad glittering chimney-tops
As she gently exhales to the sun.

Hurrying creatures run
Down the labyrinth of the sinister flower.
What is it they shun?

A dark bird falls from the sun.
It curves in a rush to the heart of the vast
Flower: the day has begun.

**D. H. Lawrence**
**(1885–1930)**

D. H. Lawrence lived abroad for much of his life,
but was in England during the First World War.

# Picnic
## July 1917

We lay and ate sweet hurt-berries
    In the bracken of Hurt Wood.
Like a quire of singers singing low
    The dark pines stood.

Behind us climbed the Surrey hills,
    Wild, wild in greenery;
At our feet the downs of Sussex broke
    To an unseen sea.

And life was bound in a still ring,
    Drowsy, and quiet, and sweet...
When heavily up the south-east wind
    The great guns beat.

We did not wince, we did not weep,
    We did not curse or pray;
We drowsily heard, and someone said,
    'They sound clear to-day'.

We did not shake with pity and pain,
    Or sicken and blanch white.
We said, 'If the wind's from over there
    There'll be rain to-night'.

Once pity we knew, and rage we knew,
    And pain we knew, too well,
As we stared and peered dizzily
    Through the gates of hell.

But now hell's gates are an old tale;
    Remote the anguish seems;
The guns are muffled and far away,
    Dreams within dreams.

And far and far are Flanders mud,
    And the pain of Picardy;
And the blood that runs there runs beyond
    The wide waste sea.

We are shut about by guarding walls:
    (We have built them lest we run
Mad from dreaming of naked fear
    And of black things done.)

We are ringed all round by guarding walls,
    So high , they shut the view.
Not all the guns that shatter the world
    Can quite break through.

Oh guns of France, oh, guns of France
    Be still, you crash in vain...
Heavily up the south wind throb
    Dull dreams of pain...

Be still, be still, south wind, lest your
    Blowing should bring the rain...
We'll lie very quiet on Hurt Hill,
    And sleep once again.

Oh, we'll lie quite still, nor listen nor look,
    While the earth's bounds reel and shake,
Lest, battered too long, our walls and we
    Should break ...should break...

**Rose Macaulay**
**(1881–1958)**

# Last Leave
## 1918

Let us forget tomorrow! For tonight
At least, with curtains drawn, and driftwood piled
On our hearthstone, we may rest, and see
The firelight flickering on familiar walls.
(How the blue flames leap when an ember falls!)

Peace, and content, and soul-security –
These are within. Without, the waste is wild
With storm-clouds sweeping by in furious flight,
And ceaseless beating of autumnal rain
Upon our window pane.

The dusk grows deeper now, the flames are low:
We do not heed the shadows, you and I,
Nor fear the grey wings of encroaching gloom,
So softly they enfold us. One last gleam
Flashes and flits, elusive as a dream,

And then dies out upon the darkened room.
So, even so, our earthly fires must die;
Yet, in our hearts, love's flame shall leap and glow
When this dear night, with all it means to me,

**Eileen Newton**
**(1883–1930)**

Eileen Newton's fiancé enlisted in the navy and was lost at sea.

# The Send-Off

Down the close, darkening lanes they sang their way
To the siding-shed,
And lined the train with faces grimly gay.

Their breasts were stuck all white with wreath and spray
As men's are, dead.

Dull porters watched them, and a casual tramp
Stood staring hard,
Sorry to miss them from the upland camp.
Then, unmoved, signals nodded, and a lamp
Winked to the guard.

So secretly, like wrongs hushed-up, they went.
They were not ours:
We never heard to which front these were sent.

Not there if they yet mock what women meant
Who gave them flowers.

Shall they return to beatings of great bells
In wild train-loads?
A few, a few, too few for drums and yells,
May creep back, to still village wells
Up half-known roads.

**Wilfred Owen**
**(1893–1918)**

# Profiteers

There are certain brisk people among us today
Whose patriotism makes quite a display.
But on closer inspection I fancy you'll find
The tools that they work with are axes to grind.

Apparently guiltless of personal greed,
They hasten to succour their country in need;
But private returns in their little top shelves
Show it's one for the country and two for themselves.

Unselfish devotion this struggle demands,
All helping each other whole heart and clean hands.
No quarter for humbugs, we want to be quit
Of men who are making, not doing their bit.

Jones challenges Brown, and Brown implicates Jones,
To the slur of self-interest nobody owns;
But each one must know at the back of his mind,
If his patriotism spells axes to grind.

**Jessie Pope**
**(1868–1941)**

# The Farmer, 1917

I see a farmer walking by himself
In a ploughed field, returning like the day
To his dark nest. The plovers circle round
In the grey sky; the blackbird calls; the thrush
Still sings – but all the rest have gone to sleep.
I see the farmer coming up the field,
Where the new corn is sown, but not yet sprung;
He seems to be the only man alive
And thinking through the twilight of this world.
I know that there is war behind those hills,
And I surmise, but cannot see the dead,
And cannot see the living in their midst –
So awfully and madly knit with death.
I cannot feel, but I know there is war,
And has been now for three eternal years,
Behind the subtle cinctures of those hills.
I see the farmer coming up the field,
And as I look, imagination lifts
The sullen veil of alternating cloud,

And I am stunned by what I see behind
His solemn and uncompromising form:
Wide hosts of men who once could walk like him
In freedom, quite alone with night and day,
Uncounted shapes of living flesh and bone,
Worn dull, quenched dry, gone blind and sick, with war;
And they are him and he is one with them;
They see him as he travels up the field.
O God, how lonely freedom seems to-day!
O single farmer walking through the world,
They bless the seed in you that earth shall reap,
When they, their countless lives, and all their thoughts,
Lie scattered by the storm: when peace shall come
With stillness, and long shivers, after death.

**Fredegond Shove**
**(1889–1949)**

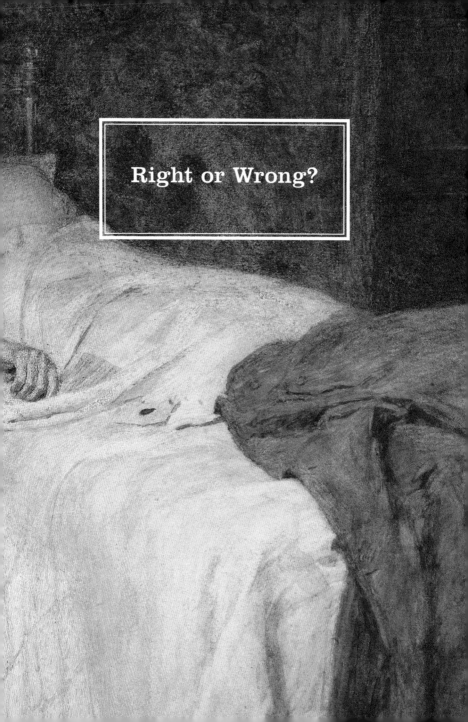

# Right or Wrong?

# The Deserter

'I'm sorry I done it, Major.'
We bandaged the livid face;
And led him, ere the wan sun rose,
To die his death of disgrace.

The bolt-heads locked to the cartridge:
The rifles steadied to rest,
As cold stock nestled to colder cheek
And foresight lined on the breast.

'*Fire!*' called the Sergeant-Major.
The muzzles flamed as he spoke:
And the shameless soul of a nameless man
Went up in cordite-smoke.

**Gilbert Frankau**
**(1884–1952)**

# To His Love

He's gone, and all our plans
    Are useless indeed.
We'll walk no more on Cotswold
    Where the sheep feed
    Quietly and take no heed.

His body that was so quick
    Is not as you
Knew it, on Severn river
    Under the blue
    Driving our small boat through.

You would not know him now...
    But still he died.
Nobly, so cover him over
    With violets of pride
    Purple from Severn side.

Cover him, cover him soon!
    And with thick-set
Masses of memoried flowers –
    Hide that red wet
    Thing I must somehow forget.

**Ivor Gurney**
**(1890–1937)**

The subject of this poem is F. W. Harvey, believed dead,
but actually a prisoner of war.

# Prisoners

Comrades of risk and rigour long ago
Who have done battle under honour's name,
Hoped (living or shot down) some meed of fame,
And wooed bright Danger for a thrilling kiss, –
Laugh, oh laugh well, that we have come to this!

Laugh, oh laugh loud, all ye who long ago
Adventure found in gallant company!
Safe in Stagnation, laugh, laugh bitterly,
While on this filthiest backwater of Time's flow
Drift we and rot, till something sets us free!

Laugh like old men with senses atrophied,
Heeding no Present, to the Future dead,
Nodding quite foolish by the warm fireside
And seeing no flame, but only in the red
And flickering embers, pictures of the past: -
Life like a cinder fading black at last.

**F. W. Harvey**
**(1888–1957)**

F. W. Harvey served in the trenches on the Western Front.
In 1916 he was taken prisoner.

# Grenadier

The Queen she sent to look for me,
    The sergeant he did say,
'Young man, a soldier will you be
    For thirteen pence a day?'

For thirteen pence a day did I
    Take off the things I wore,
And I have marched to where I lie,
    And I shall march no more.

My mouth is dry, my shirt is wet,
    My blood runs all away,
So now I shall not die in debt
    For thirteen pence a day.

To-morrow after new young men
    The sergeant he must see,
For things will all be over then
    Between the Queen and me.

And I shall have to bate my price,
    For in the grave, they say,
Is neither knowledge nor device
    Nor thirteen pence a day.

**A. E. Housman**
**(1859–1936)**

# After Court Martial

My mind is not my mind, therefore
I take no heed of what men say,
I lived ten thousand years before
God cursed the town of Nineveh.

The Present is a dream I see
Of horror and loud sufferings,
At dawn the bird will waken me
Unto my place among the kings.

And though men call me a vile name,
And all my dream companions gone,
'Tis I the soldier bears the shame,
Not I the king of Babylon.

**Francis Ledwidge**
**(1887–1917)**

# Strange Meeting

It seemed that out of battle I escaped
Down some profound tunnel, long since scooped
Through granites which titanic wars had groined.
Yet also there encumbered sleepers groaned,
Too fast in thought or death to be bestirred.
Then, as I probed them, one sprang up, and stared
With piteous recognition in fixed eyes,
Lifting distressful hands as if to bless.
And by his smile, I knew that sullen hall,
By his dead smile I knew we stood in Hell.
With a thousand pains that vision's face was grained;
Yet no blood reached there from the upper ground,
And no guns thumped, or down the flues made moan.
"Strange friend," I said, "here is no cause to mourn."
"None," said that other, "save the undone years,
The hopelessness. Whatever hope is yours,
Was my life also; I went hunting wild
After the wildest beauty in the world,
Which lies not calm in eyes, or braided hair,
But mocks the steady running of the hour,
And if it grieves, grieves richlier than here.
For of my glee might many men have laughed,

And of my weeping something had been left,
Which must die now. I mean the truth untold,
The pity of war, the pity war distilled.
Now men will go content with what we spoiled,
Or, discontent, boil bloody, and be spilled.
They will be swift with swiftness of the tigress.
None will break ranks, though nations trek from progress.
Courage was mine, and I had mystery,
Wisdom was mine, and I had mastery:
To miss the march of this retreating world
Into vain citadels that are not walled.
Then, when much blood has clogged their chariot-wheels,
I would go up and wash them from sweet wells,
Even with truths that lie too deep for taint.
I would have poured my spirit without stint
But not through wounds; not on the cess of war.
Foreheads of men have bled where no wounds were.
I am the enemy you killed, my friend.
I knew you in this dark: for so you frowned
Yesterday though me as you jabbed and killed.
I parried; but my hands were loath and cold.
Let us sleep now..."

**Wilfred Owen**
**(1893–1918)**

# Smile, Smile, Smile

Head to limp head, the sunk-eyed wounded scanned
Yesterday's Mail; the casualties (typed small)
And (large) Vast Booty from our Latest Haul.
Also, they read of Cheap Homes, not yet planned;
"For," said the paper, "When this war is done
The men's first instinct will be making homes.
Meanwhile their foremost need is aerodromes,
It being certain war has just begun.
Peace would do wrong to our undying dead, –
The sons we offered might regret they died
If we got nothing lasting in their stead.
We must be solidly indemnified.
Though all be worthy Victory which all bought,
We rulers sitting in this ancient spot
Would wrong our very selves if we forgot
The greatest glory will be theirs who fought,
Who kept this nation in integrity."
Nation? – The half-limbed readers did not chafe
But smiled at one another curiously
Like secret men who know their secret safe.
This is the thing they know and never speak,
That England one by one had fled to France,
(Not many elsewhere now save under France).
Pictures of these broad smiles appear each week,
And people in whose voice real feeling rings
Say: How they smile! They're happy now, poor things.

**Wilfred Owen**
**(1893–1918)**

This poem was written on 23 September 1918 in response
to an article in *The Mail* which showed three wounded
but smiling soldiers, under the heading 'Happy!'
News of his death reached his parents as the bells in Shrewsbury
rang to announce the Armistice on 11 November.

# Dead and Buried

I have borne my cross through Flanders,
    Through the broken heart of France,
I have borne it through the deserts of the East;
    I have wandered, faint and longing,
    Through the human hosts that, thronging,
Swarmed to glut their grinning idols with a feast.

I was crucified at Cambrai,
    And again outside Bapaume;
I was scourged for miles along the Albert Road,
    I was driven, pierced and bleeding,
    With a million maggots feeding
On the body that I carried as my load.

I have craved a cup of water,
    Just a drop to quench my thirst,
As the routed armies ran to keep the pace;
    But no soldier made reply
    As the maddened hosts swept by,
And a sweating straggler kicked me in the face.

There's no ecstasy of torture
    That the devils e'er devised,
That my soul has not endured unto the last;
    As I bore my cross of sorrow,
    For the glory of to-morrow,
Through the wilderness of battles that is passed.

Yet my heart was still unbroken,
    And my hope was still unquenched,
Till I bore my cross to Paris through the crowd.
    Soldiers pierced me on the Aisne,

But 'twas by the river Seine
That the statesmen brake my legs and made me shroud.

There they wrapped my mangled body
In fine linen of fair words,
With the perfume of a sweetly scented lie,
And they laid it in a tomb
Of the golden-mirrored room,
'Mid the many-fountained Gardens of Versailles.

With a thousand scraps of paper
They made fast the open door,
And the wise men of the Council saw it sealed.
With the seal of subtle lying,
They made certain of my dying,
Lest the torment of the peoples should be healed.

Then they set a guard of soldiers
Night and day beside the Tomb,
Where the body of the Prince of Peace is laid,
And the captains of the nations
Keep the sentries to their stations,
Lest the statesman's trust from Satan be betrayed.

For it isn't steel and iron
That men use to kill their God,
But the poison of a smooth and slimy tongue.
Steel and iron may tear the body,
But it's oily sham and shoddy
That have trampled down God's Spirit in the dung.

**Rev. G. A. Studdert Kennedy**
**(1883–1929)**

# This is no case of petty Right or Wrong

This is no case of petty right or wrong
That politicians or philosophers
Can judge. I hate not Germans, nor grow hot
With love of Englishmen, to please newspapers.
Beside my hate for one fat patriot
My hatred of the Kaiser is love true: -
A kind of god is he, banging a gong.
But I have not to choose between the two,
Or between justice and injustice. Dinned
With war and argument I read no more
Than in a storm smoking along the wind
Athwart the wood. Two witches' cauldrons roar.
From one the weather shall rise clear and gay;
Out of the other an England beautiful
And like her mother that died yesterday.
Little I know or care if, being dull,
I shall miss something that historians
Can rake out of the ashes when perchance
The phoenix broods serene above their ken.
But with the best and meanest Englishmen
I am in one crying, God save England, lest
We lose what never slaves and cattle blessed.
The ages made her that made us from dust:
She is all we know and live by, and we trust
She is good and must endure, loving her so:
And as we love ourselves we hate her foe.

**Edward Thomas**
**(1878–1917)**

An Open Ally

# A Soldier's Kiss

Only a dying horse! pull off the gear,
And slip the needless bit from frothing jaws,
Drag it aside there, leaving the road way clear,
The battery thunders on with scarce a pause.

Prone by the shell-swept highway there it lies
With quivering limbs, as fast the life-tide fails,
Dark films are closing o'er the faithful eyes
That mutely plead for aid where none avails.

Onward the battery rolls, but one there speeds
Heedlessly of comrades voices or bursting shell,
Back to the wounded friend who lonely bleeds
Beside the stony highway where he fell.

Only a dying horse! he swiftly kneels,
Lifts the limp head and hears the shivering sigh
Kisses his friend, while down his cheek there steals
Sweet pity's tear, "Goodbye old man, Goodbye".

No honours wait him, medal, badge or star,
Though scarce could war a kindlier deed unfold;
He bears within his breast, more precious far
Beyond the gift of kings, a heart of gold.

**Henry Chappell**
**(1874–1937)**

# The Turkish Trench Dog

Night held me as I crawled and scrambled near
The Turkish lines. Above, the mocking stars
Silvered the curving parapet, and clear
Cloud-latticed beams o'erflecked the land with bars;
I, crouching, lay between
Tense-listening armies, peering through the night,
Twin giants bound by tentacles unseen.
Here in dim-shadowed light
I saw him, as a sudden movement turned
His eyes towards me, glowing eyes that burned
A moment ere his snuffling muzzle found
My trail; and then as serpents mesmerize
He chained me with those unrelenting eyes,
That muscle-sliding rhythm, knit and bound
In spare-limbed symmetry, those perfect jaws
And soft-approaching pitter-patter paws.
Nearer and nearer like a wolf he crept –
That moment had my swift revolver leapt –
But terror seized me, terror born of shame
Brought flooding revelation. For he came
As one who offers comradeship deserved,
An open ally of the human race,
And sniffing at my prostrate form unnerved
He licked my face!


**Geoffrey Dearmer**
**(1893–1996)**

# Cher Ami

*Cher Ami*, how do you do!
Listen, let me talk to you;
I'll not hurt you, don't you see?
Come a little close to me.

Little scrawny blue and white
Messenger for men who fight,
Tell me of the deep, red scar,
There, just where no feathers are.

What about your poor left leg?
Tell me, *Cher Ami*, I beg.
Boys and girls are at a loss,
How you won that Silver Cross.

"The finest fun that came to me
Was when I went with Whittlesey;
We marched so fast, so far ahead!
'We all are lost,' the keeper said:

'*Mon Cher Ami* – that's my dear friend –
You are the one we'll have to send;
The whole battalion now is lost,
And you must win at any cost.'

So with the message tied on tight;
I flew up straight with all my might,
Before I got up high enough,
Those watchfull guns began to puff.

Machine-gun bullets came like rain,
You'd think I was an aeroplane;
And when I started to the rear,
My! the shot was coming near!

But on I flew, straight as a bee;
The wind could not catch up with me,
Until I dropped out of the air,
Into our own men's camp, so there!"

But, *Cher Ami*, upon my word,
You modest, modest little bird;
Now don't you know that you forgot?
Tell how your breast and leg were shot.

"Oh yes, the day we crossed the Meuse,
I flew to Rampont with the news;
Again the bullets came like hail,
I thought for sure that I should fail.

The bullets buzzed by like a bee,
So close, it almost frightened me;
One struck the feathers of this sail,
Another went right through my tail.

But when I got back to the rear,
I found they hit me, here and here;
But that is nothing, never mind;
Old *Poilu*, there is nearly blind.

I only care for what they said,
For when they saw the way I bled,
And found in front a swollen lump,
The message hanging from this stump;

The French and Mine said, '*Tres bien,*'
Or 'Very good' – American.
'*Mon Cher Ami*, you brought good news;
Our Army's gone across the Meuse!

You surely had a lucky call!
And so I'm glad. I guess that's all.
I'll sit, so pardon me, I beg;
It's hard a-standing on one leg!"

### Harry Webb Farrington
### (1879–1930)

Cher Ami served as a carrier pigeon during the autumn of 1918.
On 3 October 500 men of 'The Liberty Division' (the 77th Infantry Division)
of the American army were trapped and surrounded by enemy soldiers.
By the second day fewer than 200 were left alive or unwounded.
They sent several carrier pigeons out who failed to get through and
the American Artillery, unwittingly, began shelling their own troops.
Cher Ami was sent off with a message tied to his leg saying,
'We are along the road parallel to 276.4. Our own artillery is dropping
a barrage directly on us. For heaven's sake, stop it.' As the pigeon flew off,
the Germans opened fire, but Cher Ami managed to deliver the message
and saved the lives of the 200 soldiers. He was badly wounded and lost a leg,
but the medics saved his life. In recognition of his great bravery,
the French awarded the carrier pigeon the Croix de Guerre with Palm
for heroic service. He returned to America by boat and became one
of the heroes of the First World War.

# Break of Day in the Trenches

The darkness crumbles away.
It is the same old druid Time as ever,
Only a living thing leaps my hand,
A queer sardonic rat,
As I pull the parapet's poppy
To stick behind my ear.
Droll rat, they would shoot you if they knew
Your cosmopolitan sympathies.
Now you have touched this English hand
You will do the same to a German
Soon, no doubt, if it be your pleasure
To cross the sleeping green between.
It seems you inwardly grin as you pass
Strong eyes, fine limbs, haughty athletes,
Less chanced than you for life,
Bonds to the whims of murder,
Sprawled in the bowels of the earth,
The torn fields of France.
What do you see in our eyes
At the shrieking iron and flame
Hurled through still heavens?
What quaver – what heart aghast?
Poppies whose roots are in man's veins
Drop, and are ever dropping;
But mine in my ear is safe –
Just a little white with dust.

**Isaac Rosenberg**
**(1890–1918)**

# Horses in War Time

**Our Dumb Friends' League**
(A Society for the encouragement of kindness to animals)
**Blue Cross Fund**
(The Original Fund for helping Horses in War)
**An Appeal**

I'm only a cavalry charger,
    And I'm dying as fast as I can
(For my body is riddled with bullets –
    They've potted both me and my man);
And though I've no words to express it,
    I'm trying this message to tell
To kind folks who work for the Red Cross –
    Oh, please help the Blue one as well!

My master was one in a thousand,
    And I loved him with all this poor heart
(For horses are built just like humans,
    Be kind to them – they'll do their part);
So please send out help for our wounded,
    And give us a word in your prayers;
This isn't so strange as you'd fancy –
    The Russians do it in theirs.

PLEASE
HELP

I'm only a cavalry charger,
And my eyes are becoming quite dim
(I really don't mind, though I'm 'done for',
So long as I'm going to him);
But first I would plead for my comrades,
Who're dying and suffering too –
Oh, please help the poor wounded horses!
I'm sure that you would – if you knew.

**Help the Blue Cross hospitals in France, the Blue Cross hospitals in Italy and to supply horse comforts for the Home and Expeditionary Forces**

**'Scots Greys'**

This was part of an advertisement for the Blue Cross charity in
*The Press* on 12 January 1916.
The Royal Scots Greys began as three troops of dragoons, founded in 1678,
which amalgamated into the Royal Regiment of Scots Dragoons.
At first they were known as the Grey Dragoons, the 'Grey' referring to
the colour of the troopers' jackets, but by 1693 the regiment was also
mounted exclusively on grey horses. During the First World War
the horses were dyed dark chestnut so they did not stand out.
They served on the Western Front throughout the war.
In 1971 they were amalgamated with the 3rd Carbiniers
(Prince of Wales Dragoon Guards) to form the Royal Scots Dragoon Guards.

# Magpies in Picardy

The magpies in Picardy
Are more than I can tell.
They flicker down the dusty roads
And cast a magic spall
On the men who march through Picardy,
Through Picardy to hell.

(The blackbird flies with panic,
The swallow goes like light,
The finches move like ladies,
The owl floats by at night;
But the great and flashing magpie
He flies as artists might.)

A magpie in Picardy
Told me secret things –
Of the music in white feathers,
And the sunlight that sings
And dances in deep shadows –
He told me with his wings.

(The hawk is cruel and rigid,
He watches from a height;
The rook is slow and sombre,
The robin loves to fight;
But the great and flashing magpie
He flies as lovers might.)

He told me that in Picardy,
An age ago or more,
While all his fathers were still eggs,
These dusty highways bore
Brown singing soldiers marching out
Through Picardy to war.

He said that still through chaos
Works on the ancient plan,
And two things have altered not
Since first the world began –
The beauty of the wild green earth
And the bravery of man.

(For the sparrow flies unthinking
And quarrels in his flight;
The heron trails his legs behind,
The lark goes out of sight;
But the great and flashing magpie
He flies as poets might.)

**T. P. Cameron Wilson**
**(1889–1918)**

This was originally published in *The Westminster Gazette*
without the last two verses. General Sir Archibald
(later Field Marshall, Lord) Wavell remembered them for
his anthology *Other Men's Flowers*.

# A Thrush in the Trenches
from: *The Soldier*

Suddenly he sang across the trenches,
    vivid in the fleeting hush
as a star-shell through the smashed black branches,
    a more than English thrush.

Suddenly he sang, and those who listened
    nor moved nor wondered, but
heard, all bewitched, the sweet unhastened
    crystal Magnificat.

One crouched, a muddied rifle clasping,
    and one a filled grenade,
but little cared they, while he went lisping
    the one clear tune he had.

Paused horror, hate and Hell a moment,
    (you could almost hear the sigh)
and still he sang to them, and so went
    (suddenly) singing by.

**Humbert Wolfe**
**(1885–1940)**

Let us Remember
Spring will
Come Again

# Rural Economy

There was winter in those woods
    And still it was July:
There were Thule solitudes
    With thousands huddling nigh;
There the fox had left his den,
The scraped holes hid not stoats but men.

To these woods the rumour teemed
    Of peace five miles away;
In sight, hills hovered, houses gleamed
    Where last perhaps we lay
Till the cockerels bawled bright morning and
The hours of life slipped the slack hand.

In sight, life's farms sent forth their gear,
    Here rakes and ploughs lay still,
Yet, save some curious clods, all here
    Was raked and ploughed with a will.
The sower was the ploughman too,
And iron seeds broadcast he threw.

What husbandry could outdo this?
    With flesh and blood he fed
The planted iron that nought amiss
    Grew thick and swift and red,
And in a night though ne'er so cold
Those acres bristled a hundredfold.

Why, even the wood as well as field
    This ruseful farmer knew
Could be reduced to plough and tilled
    And if he planned, he'd do;
The field and wood, all bone-fed loam,
Shot up a roaring harvest home.

# Vlamertinghe:
# Passing the Chateau, July, 1917

'And all her silken flanks with garlands drest' –
But we are coming to the sacrifice.
Must those have flowers who are not yet gone West?
May those have flowers who live with death and lice?
This must be the floweriest place
That earth allows; the queenly face
Of the proud mansion borrows grace for grace
Spite of those brute guns lowing at the skies.

Bold great daisies, golden lights,
Bubbling roses' pinks and whites –
Such a gay carpet! poppies by the million;
Such damask! such vermilion!
But if you ask me, mate, the choice of colour
Is scarcely right; this red should have been duller.

**Edmund Blunden (both poems)**
**(1896–1974)**

# The Rainbow

*And it shall come to pass, when I bring a cloud over*
*the earth, that the bow shall be seen in the clouds.*
**Genesis, chapter ix, verse 14**

I watch the white dawn gleam
  To the thunder of hidden guns.
I hear the hot shells scream
Through skies as sweet as a dream
  Where the silver dawnbreak runs.
And stabbing of light
Scorches the virginal white.
But I feel in my being, the old, high sanctified thrill,
And I thank the gods that the dawn is beautiful still.

From death that hurtles by
  I crouch in the trench day-long,
But up to a cloudless sky
From the ground where our dead men lie
  A brown lark soars in song.
Through the tortured air,
Rent by the shrapnel's flare,
Over the troubles dead he carols his fill,
And I thank the gods that the birds are beautiful still.

Where the parapet is low
    And level with the eye
Poppies and cornflowers grow
And the corn sways to and fro
    In a pattern against the sky.
The gold stalks hide
Bodies of men who died
Charging at dawn through the dew to be killed or to kill.
I thank the gods that the flowers are beautiful still.

When night falls dark we creep
    In silence to our dead.
We dig a few feet deep
And leave them there to sleep –
    But blood at night is red,
Yea, even at night
And a dead man's face is white.
And I dry my hands, that are also trained to kill,
And I look to the stars – for the stars are beautiful still.

**Leslie Coulson**
**(1889–1916)**

Shortly before he died, Leslie Coulson wrote in a letter,
'If I should fall do not grieve for me.
I shall be one with the wind and the sun and the flowers.'

# Into Battle

The naked earth is warm with Spring,
    And with green grass and bursting trees
Leans to the sun's gaze glorying,
    And quivers in the sunny breeze;

And Life is Colour and Warmth and Light,
    And a striving evermore for these;
And he is dead who will not fight;
    And who dies fighting has increase.

The fighting man shall from the sun
    Take warmth, and life from the glowing earth;
Speed with the light-foot winds to run,
    And with the trees to newer birth;
And find, when fighting shall be done,
    Great rest, and fullness after dearth.

All the bright company of Heaven
    Hold him in their high comradeship,
The Dog-Star, and the Sisters Seven,
    Orion's Belt and sworded hip.

The woodland trees that stand together,
    They stand to him each one a friend;
They gently speak in the windy weather;
    They guide to valley and ridge's end.

The kestrel hovering by day,
    And the little owls that call by night,
Bid him be swift and keen as they,
    As keen of ear, as swift of sight.

The blackbird sings to him, 'Brother, brother,
    If this be the last song you shall sing,
Sing well, for you may not sing another;
    Brother, sing.'

In dreary doubtful waiting hours,
    Before the brazen frenzy starts,
The horses show him nobler powers;
    O patient eyes, courageous hearts!

And when the burning moment breaks,
    And all things else are out of mind,
And only Joy-of-Battle takes
    Him by the throat, and makes him blind,

Through joy and blindness he shall know,
    Not caring much to know, that still
Nor lead nor steel shall reach him, so
    That it be not the Destined Will.

The thundering line of battle stands,
    And in the air Death moans and sings:
But Day shall clasp him with strong hands,
    And Night shall fold him in soft wings.

**Julian Grenfell
(1888–1915)**

This was the last poem Julian Grenfell wrote, in April 1915,
making the lines in verse 7 particularly poignant.

# May, 1915

Let us remember Spring will come again
To the scorched, blackened woods, where the
    wounded trees
Wait, with their old wise patience for the
    heavenly rain,
Sure of the sky: sure of the sea to send its
    healing breeze,
Sure of the sun. And even as to these
Surely the Spring, when God shall please,
Will come again like a divine surprise
To those who sit to-day with their great Dead,
    hands in their hands, eyes in their eyes,
At one with Love, at one with Grief: blind to the
    scattered things and changing skies.

**Charlotte Mew**
**(1869–1928)**

# The Fields of Flanders

Last year the fields were all glad and gay
With silver daisies and silver may;
There were kingcups gold by the river's edge
And primrose stars under every hedge.

This year the fields are trampled and brown,
The hedges are broken and beaten down,
And where the primroses used to grow
Are little black crosses set in a row.

And the flower of hopes, and the flower of dreams,
The noble, fruitful, beautiful schemes,
The tree of life with its fruit and bud,
Are trampled down in the mud and the blood.

The changing seasons will bring again
The magic of Spring to our wood and plain:
Though the Spring be so green as never was seen
The crosses will still be black in the green.

The God of battles shall judge the foe
Who trampled our country and laid her low...
God! hold our hands on the reckoning day,
Lest all we owe them we should repay.

**E. Nesbit**
**(1858–1924)**

# Returning, We Hear The Larks

Sombre the night is.
And though we have our lives, we know
What sinister threat lurks there.

Dragging these anguished limbs, we only know
This poison-blasted track opens on our camp –
On a little safe sleep.

But hark! joy – joy – strange joy.
Lo! heights of night ringing with unseen larks.
Music showering our upturned list'ning faces.

Death could drop from the dark
As easily as song –
But song only dropped,
Like a blind man's dreams on the sand

By dangerous tides,
Like a girl's dark hair for she dreams no ruin
    lies there,
Or her kisses where a serpent hides.

**Isaac Rosenberg**
**(1890–1918)**

# As the Team's Head-Brass

As the team's head-brass flashed out on the turn
The lovers disappeared into the wood.
I sat among the boughs of the fallen elm
That strewed the angle of the fallow, and
Watched the plough narrowing a yellow square
Of charlock. Every time the horses turned
Instead of treading me down, the ploughman leaned
Upon the handles to say or ask a word,
About the weather, next about the war.
Scraping the share he faced towards the wood,
And screwed along the furrow till the brass flashed
Once more.
    The blizzard felled the elm whose crest
I sat in, by a woodpecker's round hole,
The ploughman said. 'When will they take it away?'
'When the war's over.' So the talk began –
One minute and an interval of ten,
A minute more and the same interval.
'Have you been out?' 'No.' 'And don't want to, perhaps?'
'If I could only come back again, I should.
I could spare an arm, I shouldn't want to lose
A leg. If I should lose my head, why, so,

I should want nothing more... Have many gone
From here?' 'Yes.' 'Many lost?' 'Yes, a good few.
Only two teams work on the farm this year.
One of my mates is dead. The second day
In France they killed him. It was back in March,
The very night of the blizzard, too. Now if
He had stayed here we should have moved the tree.'
'And I should not have sat here. Everything
Would have been different. For it would have been
Another world.' 'Ay, and a better, though
If we could see all all might seem good.' Then
The lovers came out of the wood again:
The horses started and for the last time
I watched the clods crumble and topple over
After the ploughshare and the stumbling team.

**Edward Thomas**
**(1878–1917)**

# A Listening Post

The sun's a red ball in the oak
    And all the grass is grey with dew,
Awhile ago a blackbird spoke –
    He didn't know the world's askew.

And yonder rifleman and I
    Wait here behind the misty trees
To shoot the first man that goes by,
    Our rifles ready on our knees.

How could we know that if we fail
    The world may lie in chains for years
And England be a bygone tale
    And right be wrong, and laughter tears?

Strange that this bird sits there and sings
    While we must only sit and plan –
Who are so much the higher things –
    The murder of our fellow man...

But maybe God will cause to be –
    Who brought forth sweetness from the strong –
Out of our discords harmony
    Sweeter than that bird's song.

**Robert Ernest Vernède**
**(1875–1917)**

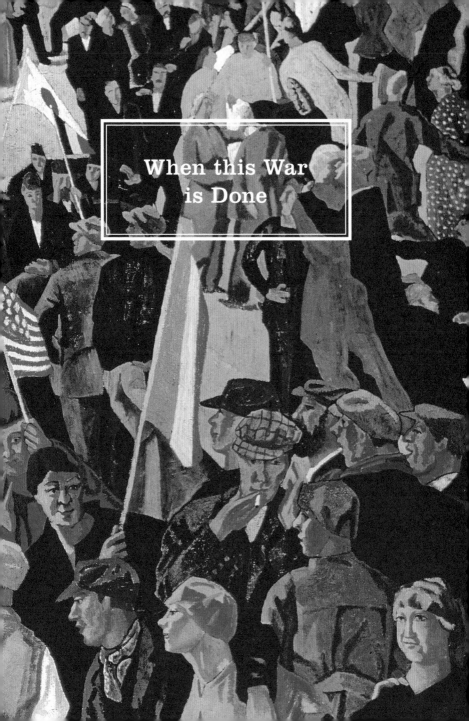

# When this War
# is Done

# When this Bloody War is Over
## To the tune of 'What a Friend I have in Jesus'

When this bloody war is over,
Oh, how happy I shall be!
When I get my civvy clothes on
No more soldiering for me.
No more church parades on Sunday,
No more asking for a pass.
I shall tell the Sergeant-Major
To stick his passes up his arse.

When this bloody war is over,
Oh, how happy I shall be.
When I get my civvy clothes on,
No more soldiering for me.
I shall sound my own revally,
I shall make my own tattoo.
No more N.C.O.s to curse me,
No more bleeding Army stew.

N.C.O.s will all be navvies,
Privates ride in motor cars.
N.C.O.s will smoke their Woodbines,
Privates puff their big cigars.
No more standing-to in trenches,
Only one more church parade.
No more shivering on the firestep,
No more Tickler's marmalade.

**Anon**

# Ypres

She was a city of patience; of proud name,
Dimmed by neglecting Time; of beauty and loss;
Of acquiescence in the creeping moss.
But on a sudden fierce destruction came
Tigerishly pouncing: thunderbolt and flame
Showered on her street, to shatter them and toss
Her ancient towers to ashes. Riven across,
She rose, dead, into never-dying fame.

White against heavens of storm, a ghost, she is known
To the world's ends. The myriads of the brave
Sleep round her. Desolately glorified,
She, moon-like, draws her own far-moving tide
Of sorrow and memory; toward her, each alone,
Glide the dark dreams that seek an English grave.

**Laurence Binyon**
**(1869–1943)**

# Armistice Day

Birds stayed not their singing,
The heart its beating,
The blood its steady coursing
    The child in the dark womb
Stirred; dust settled in the tomb.

Old wounds were still smarting,
Echoes were hollow-sounding,
New desires still upspringing.
    No silent Armistice might stay
Life and Death wrangling in the old way.

Earth's pulse still was beating,
The bright stars circling;
Only our tongues were hushing.
    While Time ticked silent on, men drew
A deeper breath than passion knew.

**John Freeman**
**(1880–1929)**

# Two Fusiliers

And have we done with War at last?
Well, we've been lucky devils both,
And there's no need of pledge or oath
To bind our lovely friendship fast,
By firmer stuff
Close bound enough.

By wire and wood and stake we're bound,
By Fricourt and by Festubert,
By whipping rain, by the sun's glare,
By all the misery and loud sound,
By a Spring day,
Bt Picard clay.

Show me the two so closely bound
As we, by the wet bond of blood,
By friendship blossoming from mud,
By Death: we faced him, and we found
Beauty in Death,
In dead men, breath.

**Robert Graves**
**(1895–1985)**

# High Wood
## 1918

Ladies and gentlemen, this is High Wood,
Called by the French, Bois des Fourneaux,
The famous spot which in Nineteen-Sixteen,
July, August and September was the scene
Of long and bitterly contested strife,
By reason of its High commanding site.
Observe the effect of shell-fire in the trees
Standing and fallen; here is the wire; this trench
For months inhabited, twelve times changed hands;
(They soon fall in), used later as a grave.
It has been said on good authority
That in the fighting for this patch of wood
Were killed somewhere above eight thousand men,
Of whom the greater part were buried here
This mound on which you stand being...

                        Madame, please,
You are requested kindly not to touch
Or take away the Company's property
As souvenirs: you'll find we have on sale
A large variety, all guaranteed.
As I was saying, all is as it was,
This is an unknown British officer,
The tunic having lately rotted off.
Please follow me – this way...

                     the *path*, sir, *please*,

The ground which was secured at great expense
The Company keeps absolutely untouched,
And in that dug-out (genuine) we provide
Refreshments at a reasonable rate.
You are requested not to leave about
Paper, or ginger-beer bottles, or orange-peel,
There are waste-paper baskets at the gate.

**Philip Johnstone**
**(1890–1968)**

This poem was first published in *The Nation*, 16 February 1918.

# The King's Pilgrimage
### King George V's Visit to War Cemeteries
### in France 1922

Our King went forth on pilgrimage
    His prayers and vows to pay
To them that saved our heritage
    And cast their own away.

And there was little show of pride
    Or prows of belted steel,
For the clean-swept oceans every side
    Lay free to every keel.

And the first land he found it, it was shoal and banky
ground – Where the broader seas begin,
And a pale tide grieving at the broken harbour-mouth
Where they worked the death-ships in.

And there was neither gull on the wing,
    Nor wave that could not tell
Of bodies that were buckled in the life-bouy's ring
    That slid from swell to swell.

*All that they had they gave – they gave; and they shall not return,*
*For these are those that have no grave where any heart may mourn.*

And the next land he found, it was low and hollow ground –
Where once the cities stood,
But the man-high thistle had been master of it all,
Or the bulrush by the flood.

And there was neither blade of grass,
    Nor lone star in the sky,
But shook to see some spirit pass
    And took its agony.

And the next land he found, it was bare and hilly ground –
Where once the bread-corn grew,
But the fields were cankered and the water was defiled,
And the trees were riven through.

    And there was neither paved highway,
        Nor secret path in the wood,
    But had borne its weight of the broken clay
        And darkened 'neath the blood.

*Father and mother they put aside, and the nearer love also –*
*An hundred thousand men that died whose graves shall no man know.*

And the last land he found, it was fair and level ground
About a carven stone,
And a stark Sword brooding on the bosom of the Cross
Where high and low are one.

    And there was grass and the living trees,
        And the flowers of the spring,
    And there lay gentlemen from out of all the seas
        That ever called him King.

*'Twixt Nieuport sands and the eastward lands where the Four Red*

*Rivers spring,*
*Five hundred thousand gentlemen of those that served*
*their King.*

All that they had they gave – they gave –
In sure and single faith.
There can no knowledge reach the grave
To make them grudge their death
Save only if they understood
That, after all was done,
We they redeemed denied their blood
And mocked the gains it won.

**Rudyard Kipling**
**(1865–1936)**

Kipling's son Jack died in the First World War and his room was preserved
as he left it. The National Trust looks after Kipling's home, Bateman's.

# Does it Matter?

Does it matter? – losing your legs? ...
For people will always be kind,
And you need not show that you mind
When others come in after hunting
To gobble their muffin and eggs.

Does it matter? – losing your sight? ...
There's such splendid work for the blind;
And people will always be kind,
As you sit on the terrace remembering
And turning your face to the light.

Do they matter? – those dreams from the pit? ...
You can drink and forget and be glad,
And people won't say that you're mad;
For they'll know that you've fought for your country,
And no one will worry a bit.

**Siegfried Sassoon**
**(1886–1967)**

We will Remember
Them

# For the Fallen

With proud thanksgiving, a mother for her children,
England mourns for her dead across the sea.
Flesh of her flesh they were, spirit of her spirit,
Fallen in the cause of the free.

Solemn drums thrill; Death august and royal
Sings sorrow up into immortal spheres,
This is music in the midst of desolation
And a glory that shines upon out tears.

They went with songs to the battle, they were young,
Straight of limb, true of eye, steady and aglow.
They were staunch to the end against odds uncounted;
They fell with their faces to the foe.

They shall not grow old, as we that are left grow old:
Age shall not weary them, nor the years condemn.
At the going down of the sun and in the morning
We will remember them.

They mingle not with their laughing comrades again;
They sit no more at familiar tables of home;
They have no lot in our labour of the day-time;
They sleep beyond England's foam.

But where our desires are and our hopes profound,
Felt as a well-spring that is hidden from sight,
To the innermost heart of their own land they are known
As the stars are known to the Night;

As the stars that shall be bright when we are dust
Moving in marches upon the heavenly plain,
As the stars that are starry in the time of our darkness,
To the end, to the end, they remain.

**Laurence Binyon**
**(1869–1943)**

Binyon wrote this poem in September 1914 while sitting by the cliffs
between Pentire Point and The Rumps. A stone plaque was erected
in 2001 to commemorate the fact and bears the inscription:

For the Fallen
Composed on these Cliffs 1914

The plaque also bears the fourth stanza of the poem.

# Perhaps –
## (To R.A L.)

Perhaps some day the sun will shine again,
 And I shall see that still the skies are blue,
And feel once more I do not live in vain,
 Although bereft of You.

Perhaps the golden meadows at my feet
 Will make the sunny hours of Spring seem gay,
And I shall find the white May blossoms sweet,
 Though You have passed away.

Perhaps the summer woods will shimmer bright,
 And crimson roses once again be fair,
And autumn harvest fields a rich delight,
 Although You are not there.

Perhaps some day I shall not shrink in pain,
 To see the passing of the dying year,
And listen to the Christmas songs again
 Although You cannot hear.

But, though kind Time may many joys renew,
 There is one greatest joy I shall not know
Again, because my heart for loss of You
 Was broken, long ago.

### Vera Brittain
### (1893–1970)

In August 1915 Vera Brittain was engaged to Roland Leighton. At Christmas
she was granted leave from her nursing duties and went to Brighton to
meet Roland off the evening boat. She waited in the Grand Hotel for a
call saying he had arrived. Next morning a call came, to say that
he had died on 23 December, of wounds sustained on the Western Front.

# 1914  V: The Soldier

If I should die, think only this of me:
    That there's some corner of a foreign field
That is for ever England. There shall be
    In that rich earth a richer dust concealed;
A dust whom England bore, shaped, made aware,
    Gave, once, her flowers to love, her ways to roam,
A body of England's, breathing English air,
    Washed by the rivers, blest by the suns of home.

And think, this heart, all evil shed away,
    A pulse in the eternal mind, no less
        Gives somewhere back the thoughts by England given;
Her sights and sounds; dreams happy as her day;
    And laughter, learnt of friends; and gentleness,
        In hearts at peace, under an English heaven.

**Rupert Brooke**
**(1887–1915)**

This is the fifth and final poem in Rupert Brooke's sonnet sequence, '1914'.
The poems were written between December 1914 and January 1915.

# Youth's Own

Out of the fields I see them pass,
    Youth's own battalion –
Like moonlight ghosting over grass –
    To dark oblivion.

They have a wintry march to go –
    Bugle and fife and drum!
With music softer than the snow –
    Fall flurrying, they come!

They have a solemn tryst to keep
    Out on a starry heath;
To fling them down, and sleep and sleep
    Beyond Reveille – Death!

Since Youth has vanished from our eyes,
    Who of us glad can be?
Who will be grieving, when he dies
    And leaves this Calvary?

**John Galsworthy**
**(1867–1933)**

# In Flanders Fields

In Flanders fields the poppies blow
Between the crosses, row on row,
    That mark our place; and in the sky
    The larks, still bravely singing, fly
Scarce heard amid the guns below.

We are the Dead. Short days ago
We lived, felt dawn, saw sunset glow,
    Loved and were loved, and now we lie,
      In Flanders fields.

Take up our quarrel with the foe:
To you from failing hands we throw
    The torch; be yours to hold it high.
    If ye break faith with us who die
We shall not sleep, though poppies grow
    In Flanders fields.

**John McCrae**
**(1872–1918)**

John McCrae was a Canadian doctor and part-time soldier before the war;
from 1914 on he worked as a field surgeon in France.
This poem was written during the Second Battle of Ypres, May 1915,
when he treated hundreds of mainly British gas victims.

# The Cenotaph

Not yet will those measureless fields be green again
Where only yesterday the wild, sweet, blood of wonderful
    youth was shed;
There is a grave whose earth must hold too long,
    too deep a stain,
Though for ever over it we may speak as proudly
    as we may tread.
But here, where the watchers by lonely hearths from the thrust
    of an inward sword have more slowly bled,
We shall build the Cenotaph: Victory, winged, with Peace,
    winged too, at the column's head.
And over the stairway, at the foot – oh! here, leave desolate,
    passionate hands to spread
Violets, roses, and laurel, with the small, sweet, twinkling
    country things
Speaking so wistfully of other Springs,
From the little gardens of the little places where son or
    sweetheart was born and bred.
In splendid sleep, with a thousand brothers
      To lovers – to mothers
      Here, too, lies he:
Under the purple, the green, the red,
It is all young life: it must break some women's hearts to see
Such a brave, gay coverlet to such a bed!
Only, when all is done and said,
God is not mocked and neither are the dead.
For this will stand in our Market-place –
      Who'll sell, who'll buy
      (Will you or I Lie to each other with the better grace)?
While looking in every busy whore's and huckster's face
As they drive their bargains, is the Face
Of God: and some young, piteous, murdered face.

**Charlotte Mew**
**(1869–1928)**

# Spring in War-Time

Now the sprinkled blackthorn snow
    Lies along the lovers' lane
Where last year we used to go –
    Where we shall not go again.

In the hedge the buds are new,
    By our wood the violets peer –
Just like last year's violets, too,
But they have no scent this year.

Every bird has heart to sing
    Of its nest, warmed by its breast;
We had heart to sing last spring,
    But we never built our nest.

Presently red roses blown
    Will make all the garden gay ...
Not yet have the daisies grown
    On your clay.

**E. Nesbit**
**(1858–1924)**

# Anthem for Doomed Youth

What passing bells for these who die as cattle?
    Only the monstrous anger of the guns.
    Only the stuttering rifles' rapid rattle
Can patter out their hasty orisons.
No mockeries now for them; no prayers nor bells,
    Nor any voice of mourning save the choirs, –
The shrill, demented choirs of wailing shells;
    And bugles calling for them from sad shires.

What candles may be held to speed them all?
    Not in the hands of boys, but in their eyes
Shall shine the holy glimmers of good-byes.
    The pallor of girls' brows shall be their pall;
Their flowers the tenderness of patient minds,
And each slow dusk a drawing-down of blinds.

**Wilfred Owen**
**(1893–1918)**

# The Tomb of the Unknown Warrior
## Westminster Abbey

Beneath this stone rests the body
of a British Warrior
unknown by name or rank
brought from France to lie among
the most illustrious of the land
and buried here on Armistice Day
11 Nov: 1920. In the presence of
His Majesty King George V
his ministers of state
the chiefs of his forces
and a vast concourse of the nation.

Thus are commemorated the many
multitudes who during the Great
War of 1914–1918 gave the most that
man can give life itself
For God
for King and Country
for loved ones home and empire
for the sacred cause of justice and
the freedom of the world.

They buried him among the kings because he
had done good toward God and toward
his house.

**Dr Herbert Ryle**
**Dean of Westminster Abbey**
**(1856–1925)**
The Tomb has now become a symbol of war dead from all conflicts and is the
only floor tomb in Westminster Abbey that is never walked on

# To One Who Was With Me
# in the War

It was too long ago – the Company which we served with ...
We call it back in visual fragments, you and I,
Who seem, ourselves, like relics casually preserved with
Our mindfulness of old bombardments when the sky
With blundering din blinked cavernous,

          Yet a sense of power
Invaded us when, recapturing an ungodly hour
Of ante-zero crisis, in one thought we've met
To stand in some redoubt of Time – to share again
All but the actual wetness of the flare-lit rain,
All but the living presences who haunt us yet
With gloom-patrolling eyes.

          Remembering, we forget
Much that was monstrous, much that clogged our souls with clay
When hours were guides who led us by the longest way –
And when the worst had been endured could still disclose
Another worst to thwart us ...

          We forget our fear ...
And, while the uncouth Event begins to lour less near,
Discern the mad magnificence whose storm-light throws
Wild shadows on these after-thoughts that send your brain
Back beyond Peace, exploring sunken ruinous roads.
Your brain, with files of flitting forms hump-backed with loads,
On its own helmet hears the tinkling drops of rain, –

Follows to an end some night-relief, and strangely sees
The quiet no-man's-land of daybreak, jagg'd with trees
That loom like giant Germans ...
                    I'll go with you then,
Since you must play this game of ghosts. At listening-posts
We'll peer across dim craters; joke with jaded men
Whose names we've long forgotten. (Stoop low there; it's the place
The sniper enfilades.) Round the next bay you'll meet
A drenched platoon-commander; chilled he drums his feet
On squelching duck-boards; winds his wrist watch, turns his head,
And shows you how you looked – your ten-years-vanished face,
Hoping the War will end next week ...
What's that you said?

**Siegfried Sassoon**
**(1886–1967)**

# When you see millions of the mouthless dead

When you see millions of the mouthless dead
Across your dreams in pale battalions go,
Say not soft things as other men have said,
That you'll remember. For you need not so.
Give them not praise. For, deaf, how should they know
It is not curses heaped upon each gashed head?
Nor tears. Their blind eyes see not your tears flow.
Nor honour. It is easy to be dead.
Say only this, 'They are dead.' Then add thereto,
'Yet many a better one has died before.'
Then, scanning all the o'ercrowded mass, should you
Perceive one face that you loved heretofore,
It is a spook. None wears the face you knew.
Great death has made all his for evermore.

**Charles Hamilton Sorley**
**(1895–1915)**

This poem was found in Charles Hamilton Sorley's kit after
his death and was probably the last that he wrote.

# A Girl's Song

The Meuse and the Marne have little waves;
The slender poplars o'er them lean.
One day they will forget the graves
That give the grass its living green

Some brown French girl the rose will wear
That springs above his comely head;
Will twine it in her russet hair,
Nor wonder why it is so red.

His blood is in the rose's veins,
His hair is in the yellow corn.
My grief is in the weeping rains
And in the keening wind forlorn.

Flow softly, softly, Marne and Meuse;
Tread lightly all ye browsing sheep;
Fall tenderly, O silver dews,
For here my dear love lies asleep.

The earth is on his sealèd eyes,
The beauty marred that was my pride;
Would I were lying where he lies,
And sleeping sweetly by his side!

The spring will come by Meuse and Marne,
The birds be blithesome in the tree.
I heap the stones to make his cairn
Where many sleep as sound as he.

**Katharine Tynan**
**(1861–1931)**

# Poets

**Robert Harold Beckh (1894–1916)** was killed in action while on patrol near Bertrancourt in France.

**Paul Bewsher (1894–1966)** joined the Royal Naval Air Force in 1914. He was shot down and awarded Distinguished Service Cross. From 1918 to 1919 he served in the RAF.

**Laurence Binyon (1869–1943)** joined the Red Cross and went to the Front as an orderly. Binyon wrote 'For the Fallen' while sitting by the cliffs between Pentire Point and The Rumps, a stretch of coast owned by the National Trust.

**Edward Blunden (1896–1974)** fought at the Somme and Ypres and was awarded the MC.

**John Graham Bower / 'Klaxon' (1886–1940)** served in the Navy. He was awarded the Distinguished Service Order and was mentioned in despatches.

**Robert Bridges (1844–1930)** was appointed Poet Laureate in 1913. He was a passionate supporter of the First World War, seeing it as a fight of good against evil.

**Vera Brittain (1893–1970)** joined the Voluntary Aid Detachment as a nurse and served in London, Malta and France. In August 1915 she was engaged to Roland Leighton. At Christmas she was granted leave from her nursing duties and went to Brighton to meet Roland off the evening boat. She waited in the Grand Hotel for a call saying he had arrived. Next morning a call came, to say that he had died of wounds sustained on the Western Front.

**Rupert Brooke (1887–1915)** joined the Royal Naval Division. He died of blood poisoning on the way to Gallipoli.

**May Wedderburn Cannan (1893–1973)** joined the Voluntary Aid Detachment, trained as a nurse and later also worked for Military Intelligence in France.

**Henry Chappell (1874–1937)** was known as the Bath Railway Poet as for many years he was a porter at Bath Station. Many of his poems were published in the *Daily Express*.

**Leslie Coulson (1889–1916)** fought in Malta, Egypt and at Gallipoli, where he was wounded. He recovered in hospital in Egypt, was sent to France and was killed in action at the Battle of the Somme. Shortly before he died, he wrote in a letter, 'If I should fall do not grieve for me. I shall be one with the wind and the sun and the flowers.'

**W. H. Davies (1871–1940)** was born in Wales and apprenticed at an early age to a picture-framer. He abandoned his training, became a vagrant and took part in the Klondike gold-rush, where he lost a leg while attempting to steal a ride on a train. He settled in London and later moved to a cottage in Kent owned by Edward Thomas.

**Jeffrey Day (1896–1918)** joined Royal Naval Air Service, and awarded a posthumous Distinguished Service Cross 'for great skill and bravery as a pilot'. He is thought to have been killed in action against six German aircraft.

**Geoffrey Dearmer (1893–1996)** fought at Gallipoli and on the Somme.

**Henry Webb Farrington (1879–1930)** was Athletic Director for French troops during the First World War.

**Gilbert Frankau (1884–1952)** fought at Loos, Ypres, on the Somme and in Italy. He was a squadron leader in the RAF in the Second World War.

**John Freeman (1880–1929)** was a poet, critic and novelist. He was troubled by a weak heart, but had a successful business career, rising to be director of an insurance firm. In 1924 he was awarded the Hawthornden prize for imaginative writing.

**John Galsworthy (1867–1933)** is probably best known for his novels which trace the fortunes of the Forsyte family. In 1929 he was awarded the Order of Merit and in 1932 he received the Nobel Prize for Literature.

**Crosbie Garstin (1887–1930)** fought on the Western Front.

**Robert Graves (1895–1985)** served in France, spending more time on active duty than almost any other war poet. He excluded his war poetry from nearly all collections published during his lifetime.

**Julian Grenfell (1888–1915)** became a regular soldier in 1910 and was awarded the Distinguished Service Order and mentioned in despatches twice. He was badly wounded by shrapnel near Ypres and died of his wounds in hospital in Boulogne.

**Ivor Gurney (1890–1937)** served in France and was wounded and then gassed during the Passchendaele offensive. He was sent home and suffered a mental breakdown soon afterwards.

**Thomas Hardy (1840–1928)** was an enthusiastic participant in the Secret Propaganda Unit early on in the war. The unit aimed to state the British viewpoint in America. The National Trust looks after his birthplace, Hardy's Cottage, and Max Gate, where he wrote much of his work, particularly his poetry.
www.nationaltrust.org.uk/hardys-cottage/
www.nationaltrust.org.uk/max-gate/

**F. W. Harvey (1888–1957)** served in the trenches on the Western Front, winning the Distinguished Conduct Medal. In 1916 he was taken prisoner.

**W. N. Hodgson (1893–1916)** served in France, was mentioned in despatches and awarded the Military Cross for bravery at Loos in 1915. He was killed on the first day of the Battle of the Somme, July 1916.

**A. E. Housman (1859–1936)** worked at the Patent Office in London and later became Professor of Latin and Greek at the University of London and then Professor of Latin at Cambridge.

**Philip Johnstone (1890–1968)** is thought to be the pseudonym of Lt John Stanley Purvis, who fought and was wounded at the Battle of the Somme.

**Rudyard Kipling (1865–1936)** was a champion of the ordinary serviceman and contributed for many years for the 'Last Post' to be sounded each night at the Menin Gate Memorial, Ypres. He was a leading force behind the burial of the Unknown Warrior in Westminster and proposed the standard inscription used in all British war cemeteries: 'Their name liveth for evermore'. The National Trust looks after Kipling's home, Bateman's. Kipling's son Jack died in the war and his room was preserved as he left it.
www.nationaltrust.org.uk/batemans/

**D. H. Lawrence (1885–1930)** lived abroad for much of his life, but was in England during the First World War.

**Francis Ledwidge (1887–1917)** was killed in action at the Battle of Passchendaele.

**Rose Macaulay (1881–1958)** worked as a nurse and landgirl from 1916 to 1916 and then in the War Office .

**John McCrae (1872–1918)** was a Canadian doctor and part-time soldier before the war; from 1914 on he worked as a field surgeon in France. In January 1918 he was appointed consultant to all the British Armies in France, but died of pneumonia before he could take up his post.

**John Masefield (1878–1967)** was declared unfit for war and volunteered as a Red Cross orderly, first in France and then on a hospital boat at Gallipoli.

**Charlotte Mew (1869–1928)** was born in London in comfortable circumstances but her father's death in 1898 left the family relatively poor. In 1923 she was awarded a Civil List Pension on the recommendation of Walter de la Mare, Thomas Hardy and John Masefield. She killed herself in 1928, fearing that the breakdown she suffered after her mother and sister died was the beginning of insanity.

**Alice Meynell (1847–1922)** achieved critical and popular acclaim for her verse. She also wrote essays and edited periodicals with her husband, Wilfred Meynell.

**E. Nesbit (1858–1924)** began her literary career writing poetry, but is best remembered for her children's stories *The Railway Children* and *The Phoenix and the Carpet*, amongst others.

**Eileen Newton (1883–1930)** lost her fiancé after he joined the navy and was killed at sea.

**Frederick Niven (1878–1944)** was brought up in Scotland, but moved to the dry interior of Canada for treatment of a lung ailment. When the First World War broke out he was rejected for military service and became a writer for the British Ministry of Information.

**Alfred Noyes (1880–1958)** went to Exeter College, Oxford, but left before completing his degree when his first volume of poetry was published. He became a successful playwright, novelist, academic and poet, always remaining faithful to Victorian literary conventions and shunning any hint of Modernism.

**Wilfred Owen (1893–1918)** was awarded the Military Cross for 'conspicuous gallantry and devotion to duty' in 1918 and was killed in action a week before the Armistice. News of his death reached his parents as the bells in Shrewsbury rang to announce the Armistice on 11 November.

**Jessie Pope (1868–1941)** was very pro the war and wrote inspiring verse, describing it as an exciting adventure, but she was despised by many soldiers, especially Wilfred Owen, who originally dedicated 'Dulce Et Decorum Est' to her.

**Edgell Rickword (1898–1982)** served on the Western Front and was awarded the Military Cross before losing an eye and being invalided out of the army.

**Isaac Rosenberg (1890–1918)** was killed in action near Arras. His body was never recovered.

**Herbert Ryle (1856–1925)** was appointed Dean of Westminster Abbey in 1910 and was a keen supporter of the idea of a tomb to an unknown warrior. He was created KCVO in 1921 and is buried in the Abbey near the tomb.

**Siegfried Sassoon (1886–1967)** was an exceptionally brave soldier, known as 'Kangers' and 'Mad Jack'. In 1916 he was awarded the Military Cross at the Somme, but by 1917 he had became an open critic of the war.

**The Scots Greys** (The Royal Scots Greys) was a heavy cavalry regiment which only used grey horses.

**Fredegond Shove (1889–1949)** was the daughter of the historian F. W. Maitland. She married Gerald Shove, a Cambridge classical scholar and spent most of her life in or near the university.

**Eric Simson (1895–1956)** joined the Royal Field Artillery in 1914 and later transferred to the Royal Flying Corps. When it was discovered in 1917 that he was colour blind he could no longer fly on operations and became a flying instructor at Montrose in Scotland. In 1918 he was awarded the Air Force Cross.

**Charles Hamilton Sorley (1895–1915)** was killed in action at the Battle of Loos.

**Rev. G. A. Studdert Kennedy (1883–1929)** was an army chaplain, working in the trenches and behind the lines. He was known as 'Woodbine Willie' because he always carried cigarettes for the troops. He gave powerful, unconventional sermons and was awarded the Military Cross.

**Edward Thomas (1878–1917)** was killed in action at the Battle of Arras.

**Katharine Tynan (1861–1931)** was born in County Dublin. She was a strong supporter of the war and had two sons serving on the front line.

**Robert Ernest Vernède (1875–1917)** was wounded at the Somme, but returned to the Front after turning down a job at the War Office. He was killed in action at Havrincourt Wood.

**Arthur Graeme West (1891–1917)** was killed by sniper fire at Bapaume.

**Theodore P. Cameron Wilson (1889–1918)** was killed in action near Bertincourt.

**Humbert Wolfe (1885–1940)** was a prolific and popular author, writing novels and essays as well as poetry. He worked in the Civil Service and was awarded a CBE and then a CB.

**W. B. Yeats (1865–1939)** edited *The Oxford Book of Modern Verse* 1892–1935 and excluded nearly all the War Poets because he felt 'passive suffering is not a theme for poetry'. Julian Grenfell's 'Into Battle' was one of the few exceptions.

**Edward Hilton Young (1879–1960)** joined the RNVR in 1914 and was awarded the Distinguished Service Cross for service in Flanders. Wounded at Zeebrugge in 1918, he was later awarded the Distinguished Service Order for service on the Archangel front against the Bolsheviks.

**The Tomb of the Unknown Warrior** was the idea of Rev. David Railton, who had served on the Western Front. After the war he suggested the idea to Dr. Herbert Ryle, as he had decided the Abbey was the most suitable place for the tomb. With strict anonymity the body of a British soldier was chosen from amongst the thousands who had been buried at the Somme, the Aisne, Arras and Ypres. The Tomb has now become a symbol of war dead from all conflicts and is the only floor tomb in the Abbey which is never walked on.

# Index of Poets

# Index of Titles

# Acknowledgements

## Poems

Vera Brittain's 'Perhaps' is included by permission of Mark Bostridge and T.J. Brittain-Catlin, Literary Executors for the Vera Brittain Estate 1970. **May Wedderburn Cannan**, 'Lamplight' © Clars M Abrahams. **Geoffrey Dearmer**, 'The Turkish Trench Dog' © Juliet Woollcombe. **Edmund Blunden**, 'Rural Economy', 'The Zonnebeke Road' and 'Vlamertinghe' © Carcanet Press Ltd. From *SelectedPoems* (1986) edited by Robyn Marsack. **Gilbert Frankau**, 'The Deserter' © A P Watt at United Agents on behalf of Timothy d'Arch Smith. **Robert Graves**, 'Two Fusiliers' © Carcanet Press Ltd. From *Complete Poems in One Volume*, (2000) edited by Patrick Quinn. Reprinted by kind permission of his daughter, Jane Grubb. **Edgell Rickword**, 'Moonrise Over Battlefield' © Carcanet Press Ltd. From *Collected Poems* (1991) edited by Charles Hobday. **Edward Hilton-Young**, later Lord Kennet, 'Mine-Sweeping Trawlers'. Reprinted by kind permission of Lady Kennet. **F. W. Harvey**, 'Prisoners' © Eileen Griffiths. Reproduced from *F.W. Harvey Selected Poems*, edited by Anthony Boden and R. K. R. Thornton, Douglas McLean Publishing. **Dame Rose Macaulay**, 'Many Sisters and Many Brothers' and 'Picnic' © The Society of Authors as the Literary Representative of the Estate of Dame Rose Macaulay. **John Masefield**, extract from 'August 1914' © The Society of Authors as the Literary Representative of the Estate of John Masefield. **Alfred Noyes**, 'Search Lights' © The Society of Authors as the Literary Representative of the Estate of Alfred Noyes. **Siegfried Sassoon**, 'Attack', 'Does it Matter?' and 'To One Who was With Me in the War' all © Siegfried Sassoon by kind permission of the Estate of George Sassoon.

## Picture Credits

**p 9** 'The Arrival' by Bernard Meninsky, 1918, Ministry of Information Commission, © IWM; **pp 10–11** 'Volunteers Drilling in the Courtyard of Burlington House', Andrew Carrick Gow, 1915, © IWM; **p 21** 'Follow Me! Your Country Needs You', E. J. Kealey, 1914, © IWM; **p 30–31** 'Reliefs at Dawn', from *British Artists at the Front*, *Continuation of The Western Front*, 1918 (colour litho), Nevinson, Christopher Richard Wynne (1889–1946), Private Collection, The Stapleton Collection , The Bridgeman Art Library; **p 33** 'In an Ambulance', Olive Mudie-Cooke, © IWM; **p 46–47** 'L'Enfer', Georges Leroux, 1921, © IWM; **p 49** 'Evening, After a Push', Colin U. Gill, 1919, Ministry of Information Commission, © IWM; **pp 54–55** 'An Air Fight, France', Harold Wyllie, 1920, © IWM; **p 61** 'The First Zeppelin Seen from Piccadilly Circus', Andrew Carrick Gow, 1915, © IWM; **p 66** 'An Impression of Lens, France, Seen from an Aeroplane: The Anglo-German Front Line', Richard C. Carline, 1918, © IWM; **pp 68–69** 'A Destroyer Torpedoed (HMS *Ullswater*)', Charles Pears, 1918, Imperial War Museum Naval Section Commission, © The Royal Society of Marine Artists; **pp 72–73** 'A Destroyer in a Heavy Sea: From HMS *Melampus*', Philip Connard, 1918, © IWM; **pp 79** 'A Deck Hand, North Sea Patrol', Sir John Lavery, 1917, © IWM; **pp 80–81** 'Victoria Station, District Railway', Bernard Meninsky, 1918, © IWM; **p 87** 'Women's Royal Naval Service', Joyce Dennys, © IWM; **pp 90–91** 'The Balloon Apron', Frank Dobson, 1918, © IWM; **pp 102–103** 'The Last Message', William Hatherell, 1918, © IWM; **p 105** 'The Deserter', William Orpen, 1917, © IWM; **p 109** 'Oppy Wood, 1917', Nash, John Northcote, Imperial War Museum, London, UK, The Bridgeman Art Library; **p 115** 'A Wounded Soldier', Olive Mudie-Cooke, © IWM; **pp 118–119** 'Convalescent Horses from a Veterinary Hospital being Exercised, attached to a Long Rope', Edwin Noble, © IWM; **p 127** 'Blue Cross Fund', YIM, 1915, © IWM; **pp 132–133** 'The 42nd Casualty Clearing Station, Douai', Edwin Martin, 1919, © IWM; **pp 158–159** 'The interior of the dining room of the Star and Garter hotel in Richmond', J Hodgson Lobley, 1918, © IWM; **pp 160–161** 'In Flanders Fields', 1919, illustration after original by Willy Werner in Hindenburg-Denkmal (Hindenburg Monument), Mary Evans Picture Library; **p 169** 'Whitehall: The Cenotaph', Illustration by H. M. Livens in E. V. Lucas, *London*, 1926, Mary Evans Picture Library; **p 173** 'To the Unknown British Soldier in France', Willian Orpen, 1921, © IWM.